Safe Seeds

Settled: overcoming self, sacred cows, Pharisees, heretics & weak-kneed false prophets by scrutinizing my own spiritual heritage & riding the elusive silver bullet to the Promised Land

Dave Harris

Lyle,
I'm privileged
to watch your life's
faithfulness!
Dave Harris
1/2019

DAVE HARRIS

ISBN-13: 978-1-7926-1612-9

CONTENTS

1 Purposeful expression

Why am I writing this?

Over seven-plus decades a big, fat, mixed-up boatload of high-minded and low-brow, sanctimonious pontifications or pearls of heavenly truths have bombarded my consciousness. Which do I pursue, and which do I flush?

Questions like the following:

Who's right? Free-will Arminians or God's Sovereignty Calvinists?

Which form of baptism does one pursue as essential, or can one ignore baptism altogether?

Must I submit to authoritative (as opposed to authoritarian) leadership, or can I triumph in life independently, relying on guidance from the Holy Spirit alone?

What is the role of works in the New Testament? How does God regard earning favor versus effort?

Are there modern-day apostles?

Why do Mormons and Jehovah's Witnesses keep knocking on my door, and what do I say to them?

I'm a senior citizen. Is my work finished?

I offer you a pearl of great price: I've tripped over the best answer to some, not all, of these questions.

The good news: it doesn't matter as much as you might think. In this book I reveal the most profound solution. Warning: you won't find it on the last page. I've imbedded it in the bowels of the book to inspire you to go on a treasure hunt. You will find it and rejoice, but only if you read the whole book!

Meanwhile, what you believe may be **unsafe**.

Unsafe: trying to be good enough to make it to Heaven.
See Ephesians 2:8-9—"not of works."

Unsafe: being "elder brother" rather than the Prodigal.
See Chapter 27.

Unsafe: qualifying, minimizing, excusing or defining your sin with a loophole. See Chapters 10, 11 and 12.

Unsafe: a blind eye to false religions or ritual in the name of "tolerance." See Chapters 2 and 26.**Unsafe: Unborn whose parents ignore the Bible.** See Chapter 13.

Unsafe: being often offended. See Chapter 90.

Unsafe: religion.

GOSPEL...OR RELIGION? [Paul] had trusted religion, but when he met Jesus Christ, he got rid of all his religion. But there rose up certain of the sect of the Pharisees which believed, saying, That it was needful to circumcise them, and to command them to keep the law of Moses [Acts 15:5]. They wanted to add something to the gospel. Friend, whenever you add something to the gospel, you no longer have the gospel but you have a religion. You no longer have the gospel of Jesus Christ. The only approach that you can make to Jesus Christ is by faith. We must all come to Him by faith. He won't let us come any other way. Jesus said, "… I am the way, the truth, and the life: no man cometh unto the Father, but by me" (John 14:6). He's bottled the whole world into this. There is only one question God asks the lost world: "What do you do with My Son who died for you?" God doesn't give us some little Sunday school lesson by saying, "I want you to be a good boy. I want you to join a church. I want you to go through this and that ritual." That kind of teaching is only for an insipid religion. It does not come from God. God is saying, "My Son died for you. What will you do with Him?" The answer to that question will determine your eternal destiny. This is the issue being discussed at the council in Jerusalem. This is really exciting.

McGee, J. Vernon. Thru the Bible Commentary, Volumes 1-5: Genesis through Revelation (p. 3120). Thomas Nelson. Kindle Edition.

Perhaps like you, I have doubts, insecurities, weaknesses and strengths. I have the mechanical ability of a walnut, unlike Dad. He wanted me to watch him on service calls, but it was too wet, too dark, too cold, and I just wanted to huddle in the truck.

So, I read to understand more about what I want to write. I find that others write eloquently about which I want to write. It's not for lack of my own ideas. As a kid, I started having ideas, most of which have taken on flesh. I thought of being in a movie. Oh, not acting (although I thought about what that would be like).

My idea: I'm surrounded by the movie. It's like I'm physically in the setting. I feel like I can reach out and pick up props. Guess what? You can do that now with virtual reality or holograms.

Another idea: sit around a table in a car that drives itself. Again, it's happened. Add to that roads that never ice up because they have heating elements. Another reality though, like the others, in a limited way.

During graduate school in Denver, I attended a governmental briefing on a transportation concept. City fathers wanted an elevated train with cars that would peel off and take just you to your neighborhood. Forty years later, I don't think it happened, but it could.

So again, why am I writing this? To capture the meaningful concepts that I've thought about or read about in just 74 years. I want to capture these concepts, those of others and my own if possible, for my family and friends to chew on. They can agree or challenge me with backing for their disagreement. But from a sometimes rocky, sometimes loving first half of my life, I've learned some things that I want to pass along.

I'm searching for incentives to entice my loved ones to consider them. Some of these concepts are life-and-death. I want my family members to at least know the issues, the consequences and the joyful solutions. They can reject what I've discovered as truth, but after reading and pondering this, the rejection wouldn't come from ignorance.

Can I pull this off? Oh…how I so fervently hope so.

Oh! One more thought: some biblical passages may make multiple appearances. As someone once said, "There is only one correct interpretation…but many applications.

2 Double bubble

Many denominations, I've found, teach of a "Second Blessing" after salvation. They may call it something else.

I have heard it variously called the Baptism of the Holy Spirit, Baptism of Power, Entire Sanctification, Consecration, Confirmation.

As someone exposed to a number of evangelical denominations and who even studied Catholic doctrine as a 20-year-old, I've sought them all, to cover all the bases! The insight from each has enlightened me: Presbyterian, United Church of Christ and Catholic men of the cloth all participated in my Air Force sprinkling in Korea after I passed the test of easily finding Habukkuk, Amos and Zechariah. And Titus and Philemon.

But my preacher asked me if I wanted to be sprinkled in the morning chapel with the most people. I declined and asked for a smaller group in the Sunday night service. It happened.

Years later I felt bad that I ducked a strong declaration of my faith in front of everybody. So stateside, I asked to be dunked at Lighthouse Tabernacle. Pastor Dave held me down until I bubbled. Says Jim Nardo (having grown up with Double Bubble bubble gum): "You had a Double-Bubble baptism!"

Guilty as charged, and full of joy about it.

Safe Sects Sense

Dad liked the Salvation Army, which didn't allow baptisms. They said it divided people.

These days, I see many churches accepting whatever mode you or your parents chose for you. I don't like the idea of avoiding it altogether. After all, Jesus commanded it.

Upshot

I pointed out to the Mormon on my doorstep that their works-based religion went against the Bible: "For it is by grace you have been saved, through faith—and this is not from yourselves, it is the gift of God—not by works, so that no one can boast." Ephesians 2:8-9 (NIV)

"Is baptism a work?" the Mormon responded.

"Yes, but it isn't a requirement of salvation," I said, asking him to consider the thief on the cross. I could have added Romans 10:9-10 and John 3:16.

Conclusion: while not required for salvation, the Safe Sects answer is to follow Jesus' example in obedience.

"Plunge in today and be made complete," to borrow a phrase from the beloved hymn. The Safe Sects mode is immersion, emulating the concept of burial with Jesus.

But if you've been sprinkled 'til you're wrinkled, don't fret!

On a lighter note, I spoke at a Presbyterian church. I had a case of dry mouth, and I noticed a chalice with water, and I drank it.

A dear lady later told me she wanted to pull me off the platform. "Why?"

"You drank the baptistry!"

3 Optimist, pessimist or realist?

I have a friend I call a pessimist. He's eager to predict defeat of his favorite sports teams or political candidate.

"They might as well plow up that football field and plant corn!"

He says he's not a pessimist but, rather, a realist.

Safe Sects Sense

For the first half of my life I was taught, "Don't focus on your strengths. Focus on your weaknesses and improve them." I was constantly defeated, fired, negative. Then I learned such well-intentioned advice was all wrong, and I was instead to focus on my strengths. Success. Joy. Triumph over challenges.

Upshot

Don't try this at home, but come to think of it, by thinking the worst, my pessimistic friend ends up waking up every day to boatloads of pleasant surprises!

4 'I don't care if you dance, as long as your partner is the Holy Spirit'

I never learned how to dance. Please don't ask me. For one thing, I have no motor skills. Walruses dance more gracefully than I.

When I attended junior high school, I dreaded the monthly march over to the girls' gym where my partner corresponded to my place in line. The faculty wanted us to learn ballroom dancing.

I awkwardly held the girl at arm's length. The prettiest girl counseled me that I didn't hold her close enough!

When Mom found out about my monthly ordeal, she sent a note excusing me from such a practice, "because of our religion."

The gym teacher embarrassed me in front of all my short-pants peers.

"What is your religion?"

"Uh…Covenant."

While my schoolmates held lovelies in their arms, the gym teacher banished me to the library to write a report on badminton.

I don't know which was worse.

Safe Sects Sense

I heard a girl testify in church that a dance was a poor social mixer. Her dad, the pastor, perhaps, encouraged her say that.

I know, a passionate embrace stirs a young person's raging hormones.

Lately, I've seen beautiful dancing in a Baptist church, much along the line of ballet, expressions of praise.

I see nothing in God's Word that discourages dancing. I do see warnings against caving in to the influences and images of a polluted culture with rap and lyrics that glorify evil and self-centeredness.

Pentecostals occasionally celebrate with spontaneous dance. When I interviewed Leonard Olsen for the 100-year history of Christ Memorial Church, he said he was convinced of the genuineness of ecstatic dance in the 1920s when he observed a number of worshipers strewn all over the floor and someone dancing with eyes closed. He was sure the dancer would trip over the worshipers. He became a believer after the dance concluded with no casualties.

"The most valuable thing the Psalms do for me is to express the same delight in God which made David dance." C.S. Lewis

5 How to ruin your kids

I've seen it. I've felt it.

People fawn over the captivating little princess or the radiant, pint-size boy.

"Oh, isn't she the loveliest little beauty you've ever seen?"

As the eldest child, I was the cutest kid.

Until brother Thom arrived three years later.

I lost top billing.

Family and friends told him he was the best-looking child.

I admit it. I resented him. I made him cry. At every opportunity.

I took on the role of the black sheep in the family. The rebel.

Thom reinforced their admiration by complying to everyone's ideal of the model child, devoted to Mom, Dad and Jesus.

Please don't get me wrong. None of this was Thom's fault. I love him as if he were my own brother (uh, he is). Thom shouldn't have changed his behavior a bit. I wish I were more like him.

Perhaps family and friends didn't know any better.

I don't tell him this, but I admire Thom and his devotion to God, family and country. He's a teacher and an example. In many ways he's lived the life I wish I had.

I ask Suzanne how she loves her children and grandchildren.

"I love them all equally. I love them in different ways, because each has a unique personality."

No kid and no parent comes with an instruction book (other than God's Word, which teaches by Christ's example how to be unoffendable and what true success is).

Safe Sects Sense

Never compliment a child (or adult) on his or her looks. Commend one's character. Why? An Ugly Duckling is listening.

"One way we 'provoke our children' is by showing favoritism."
–Greg Laurie

For God does not show favoritism. Romans 2:11 (NIV)

Upshot

She would know who I'm talking about, but an unnamed* woman I know convinced herself she was least favored among her siblings. Other siblings thought differently.

Many years later her brother told her she was most favored, because she had written him nearly every day when he served overseas with the military in a lonely, isolated place. He eagerly looked forward to her letters, and her soothing words made his assignment bearable.

*Unnamed? Ha! Journalists frequently use this word. She actually had a name! I'm reminded of the officer who asked the wounded soldier on the battlefield what his name was. The soldier only groaned.

Impatient, the officer pleaded, "Soldier tell me your name! I need to tell your mother!"

"My mother already knows my name!"

6 In what ways do we duck objective truth?

I can think of a number of universal, objective truths. What?

Your professor may have told you otherwise: She may have told you that truth is relative, that truth is what you think is truth.

"There are no objective truths," she told you.

Here are three proofs she was wrong:

1. In telling you that, she wanted you to consider what she said as an objective truth.

2. Try telling your banker that all truth is relative. You don't believe it yourself when you go to your company and tell them your paycheck was wrong or you have more vacation coming than their statement said.

3. Signing a contract—buying a house or car—is senseless without objective truth.

We discover many other objective truths, such as smoking is bad for me, as is substance abuse, overeating, cheating on your spouse (even your future spouse), greed, theft, hurting someone through gossip, slander or other false statements, cheating on taxes, accepting a full day's pay without working for it. The list goes on.

Why do we do things that hurt ourselves or others?

Psychologists call it dissociation. We dissociate from objective truth. Whenever we turn our backs on truth, we harm someone.

When we dissociate from Truth, we discover consequences—sometimes tragic, long-lasting consequences, and perhaps permanent damage.

My brother-in-law, John, puts it this way: By dissociating and removing our thoughts from the "yoke" of Truth (Jesus: "Take my yoke upon you, and learn of me …"), we open up our thinking to associate with the realm of fantasy occupied by lying principalities, demonic forces and rulers of this present darkness who are out to steal, kill and destroy — first ourselves, then through our shame and contempt bringing further destruction into the lives of others.

Safe Sects Sense

It's best, of course, not to dissociate from truth in the first place, but according to the ancient Book of Romans, we all dissociate and fall short of truth.

Upshot

Unless you and I change our minds, admit our shortcomings and do an about-face, first we fall, then society crumbles, and finally, the world collapses. But there's hope! My prayer is that hope jumps out at you in this book and makes you hungry for the Book and a heart-to-heart relationship with its Author.

7 Either a massive stroke or a bash in the head

At church, I befriended Dan Koser. I had seen him in maroon shorts and matching beanie. He was bigger than kids his age. He was in first grade, and I was a year ahead of him. We didn't hit it off until I was in fourth grade when he invited me over to his house. The folks dropped me off and the exuberant kid grabbed me and lifted me off the ground.

Dan recalls a turning point in my life in fourth grade. We played T-ball, and Tommy Blevins was up. He hit a fly ball, I thought, into the outfield. Suddenly everything went black, and I was on the ground bleeding between the eyes. Did the ball curve around and hit me? Nope. It was Tommy's flying bat.

The next thing I remember was that my beloved teacher, Mr. Patillo, was carrying me, running to the office.

Meanwhile, a boy stranger came up to Brother Thom and assured him that I would be OK, saying, "We need to pray for your brother."

Principal Neutzman called Mom and they swung by the house to pick her up with me in the back of Mr. Patillo's Studebaker. Off to the doctor for stitches.

Sixty years later, with aortic valve stenosis, I needed a cardiologist's clearance before undergoing deviated septum surgery. At the same time, a Navy hearing specialist referred me to a Navy neurologist, because of a wide hearing difference in my ears. Two MRIs and a CT scan followed. The neurologist called me in, showed me a picture of my brain with an inner core coated with white ischemic material.

"You either had a major stroke, or you were bashed in the head—decades ago," she said.

"That was when Tommy Blevins threw his bat at my head in fourth grade!"

She gave me some mental tests. "What is this?"

"A rhino," I said, confidently.

After some simple math problems, she said that all the synapses had reattached and there were no symptoms.

One of many miracles and near-misses.

Safe Sects Sense

For you formed my inward parts;
you knitted me together in my mother's womb.
I praise you, for I am fearfully and wonderfully made.
Wonderful are your works; my soul knows it very well.
My frame was not hidden from you,
when I was being made in secret,
intricately woven in the depths of the earth.
Your eyes saw my unformed substance;
in your book were written, every one of them,
the days that were formed for me,
when as yet there was none of them. Psalm 139:13-16 (ESV)

8 Cotton balls for a voice

Toward the end of my junior year, Mrs. Rood asked me to write a senior prophecy to be read at the junior-senior banquet for the upper classmen.

I wrote it as broadcast, thinking I would perform as one of two broadcasters. The planning committee asked Mrs. Rood which girl should be one of the broadcasters. She selected someone.

Thinking I was out of earshot, planners assumed my role as the other broadcaster and mentioned my name to Mrs. Rood.

"No, Dave mumbles," I heard her say, but my classmates insisted and prevailed.

Of course, such a comment devastated me. I had already heard a number of comments in various life situations, especially sports, that gave me an inferiority complex.

But not this time. Decades later, I heard Dad preach a sermon during which he confessed that God had given him cotton balls for a voice. I inherited that voice. But upon overhearing Mrs. Rood, I determined to over-enunciate from then on.

Of course, one can go to the other extreme and fall in love with his or her own voice, or say outlandish, inappropriate things for attention. Guilty as charged.

An early temptation of mine: hearing high-church or lukewarm Christians with foul mouths or bathroom language and thinking how cool it would be to tell a shady story or use risqué words for shock value.

Best to heed the counsel I received decades ago: "profanity is ignorance made audible."

Safe Sects Sense

But avoid irreverent babble, for it will lead people into more and more ungodliness.

2 Timothy 2:16 (ESV)

Let there be no filthiness nor foolish talk nor crude joking, which are out of place, but instead let there be thanksgiving. Ephesians 5:4 (ESV)

Everyone should be quick to listen, slow to speak and slow to become angry. James 1:19 (NIV)

9 It takes two to tango?

I've been divorced.

Twice…

…In a culture that doesn't believe in divorce—except in rare circumstances. Even then (e.g., sexual immorality [unfaithfulness], abandonment), it's not required.

Preferred (scripturally): repentance and God-enabled transformation.

Fortunately, Suzanne and I are looking forward to our fifth decade together.

Before marrying her, I took a battery of tests with a Christian counselor. I had asked him, "What's wrong with me?"

"You're a poor picker," he concluded after several months.

That's not to imply something wrong with the first two.

One could make a case that, were I thinking straight, I could have detected incompatibility from the start.

Did they have grounds to kick me out?

Having known austerity in material goods, one could identify me as a tightwad.

Self-centered.

Here's some irony: In Japan, the base hobby shop set up an audio-tape studio, complete with fancy dubbing recorders and a library of tapes one could copy in any musical genre.

Choral groups such as the Norman Luboff Choir and Ray Conniff Singers fascinating me with their love songs sung in exquisite harmony.

I fooled myself into thinking myself a romantic lover-boy by reproducing the tapes for future evenings of enthralling playback.

I failed to count the cost.

Oh, the fees didn't amount to much—a couple bucks for a blank tape.

But I spent a huge share of my spare time at the studio, leaving wife to manage two tiny kids alone for a total of dozens, maybe hundreds of hours.

My bad.

After learning the devastating consequences after my isolated tour of duty in Korea, my Air Force colleagues provided no comfort, even without knowing the circumstances—whether their taunting applied or not.

Crushed by my divorce, I poured out my heart to the colonel next door.

"Well, you know what they say: absence makes the heart grow fonder—for somebody else." That was his opinion. Not the way I conduct my life, and no way to comfort someone.

A little advice from "friends" goes a long way.

I've since learned the best question one can ask himself or herself: would I want to be married to me?

Safe Sects Sense

The Bible gives two clear grounds for divorce: (1) sexual immorality (Matthew 5:32; 19:9) and (2) abandonment by an unbeliever (1 Corinthians 7:15). Even in these two instances, though, divorce is not required or even encouraged. The most that can be said is that sexual immorality and abandonment are grounds (an allowance) for divorce. Confession, forgiveness, reconciliation, and restoration are always the first steps. Divorce should only be viewed as a last resort.

Are there any grounds for divorce beyond what the Bible explicitly says? Perhaps, but we do not presume upon the Word of God. It is very dangerous to go beyond what the Bible says (1 Corinthians 4:6). The most frequent additional grounds for divorce that people inquire about are spousal abuse (emotional or physical), child abuse, addiction to pornography, drug/alcohol use, crime/imprisonment, and mismanagement of finances (such as through a gambling addiction). None of these can be claimed to be explicit biblical grounds for a divorce.

That does not necessarily mean, though, that none of them are grounds for divorce which God would approve of. For example, we cannot imagine that it would be God's desire for a wife to remain with a husband who physically abuses her and/or their children. In such an instance, the wife should definitely separate herself and the children from the abusive husband.

However, even in such a situation, a time of separation with the goal of repentance and restoration should be the ideal, not necessarily immediately beginning divorce proceedings. Please understand, by saying that the above are not biblical grounds for divorce, we are definitely not saying that a man/woman whose spouse is engaging in such activities should remain in the situation. If there is any risk to self or children, separation is a good and appropriate step. —From *GotQuestions.org*

"Frequent abuse could also be included in the definition of marital unfaithfulness."

– Commentary from *Fire Bible*, p. 1564.

10 Trouble with logic? Use a loophole

Too many causes, and even some church doctrines, have a ready escape clause—a loophole—when things don't turn out as desired.

Sometimes the loophole stretches the truth or morphs into a euphemism—renaming an unpleasant concept into something that will tickle the ears or appears as a spoonful of sugar that makes the medicine go down.

It's not "pro-abortion." It's "pro-choice."

It's not "anti-abortion." It's "pro-life."

Another example: global warming. No matter which side you're on, you have loopholes.

If the earth doesn't cooperate with your scary stories of inundation, you transform the name from global warming to climate change.

Conversely, if you're a climate-change denier, your loophole is pointing to models that predicted the oceans would swallow cities in bygone years.

I've attended holiness churches that taught that one could achieve total eradication from sin by means of entire sanctification, or a second blessing at the altar.

I know many of these people as godly folks. Some say they no longer sin.

And yet, I've observed sin in their lives.

Loophole: define sin out of their lives—John Wesley defines sin as "a willful transgression of a known law of God." But, then, why were there sacrifices for "unintentional sins"?

An entirely sanctified sister loses her temper in traffic, or worse, at a romantic rival in the next pew. She's seething. Throw in jealous. Sprinkle in a little gossip.

But she didn't sin, according to Wesley's definition.

Loophole: Dredge up a Bible verse—"be angry and do not sin."

Loophole: Find a Bible translation that calls sins "mistakes."

"Indeed, we all make many mistakes." James 3:2 (New Living Translation)

Before you look down your nose, think of when you've used a loophole.

My favorite:

"Son, did you soil your diaper?"
Loophole: "No, my sister did it." Actually said!

Safe Sects Sense

If we say we have no sin, we deceive ourselves, and the truth is not in us. If we confess our sins, he is faithful and just to forgive us our sins and to cleanse us from all unrighteousness. If we say we have not sinned, we make him a liar, and his word is not in us. 1 John 1:8-10 (ESV)

11 More loopholes?

Dad recalled Bible studies aboard ship, and his shipmates helped settle doctrine for him, especially that of eternal security. Wesleyan Methodists generally believe as Arminians—the danger of apostasy and falling from grace in the sense of turning one's back on his or her salvation—rather than hard-core Calvinists, often characterized as "once saved, always saved." They perhaps would clarify, adding "once truly saved, always saved," and as Dad would say, hobby-horsing on predestination, whereas Wesley likely would characterize predestination as an outgrowth of God's foreknowledge of our acceptance of the gospel.

Dad noticed, to his sorrow, that the Calvinists were the first ones who strayed into the brothels while ashore.

Years later, a friend, tears streaming down his cheeks, said about the idea of predestining souls to be saved or lost, said, "I don't believe God made cookies to burn."

Sounds like a good place to follow with a loophole, this from a respected theologian:

Quite commonly people will agree that God predestines some to be saved, but they will say that he does this by looking into the future and seeing who will believe in Christ and who will not. If he sees that a person is going to come to saving faith, then he will predestine that person to be saved, based on foreknowledge of that person's faith. If he sees that a person will not come to saving faith, then he does not predestine that person to be saved. In this way, it is thought, the ultimate reason why some are saved and some are not lies within the people themselves, not within God. All that God does in his predestining work is to give confirmation to the decision he knows people will make on their own. The verse commonly used to support this view is Romans 8:29: "For those whom he foreknew he also predestined to be conformed to the image of his Son.

But this verse can hardly be used to demonstrate that God based his predestination on foreknowledge of the fact that a person would believe. The passage speaks rather of the fact that God knew persons ("those whom he foreknew"), not that he knew some fact about them, such as the fact that they would believe. —Systematic Theology: An Introduction to Biblical Doctrine (Making Sense of Series) by Wayne A. Grudem

Really? Omniscient God, who knows the end from the beginning, didn't know whether I would believe or not? His foreknowledge was limited? That's not the God I know.

Safe Sects Sense

Author Michael Wells helped settle it for me:

A pastor from England once reminded me of Matthew 7:13, 14: "Enter by the narrow gate; for the gate is wide, and the way is broad that leads to destruction, and many are those who enter by it. For the gate is small, and the way is narrow that leads to life, and few are those who find it." He explained that on this narrow way that leads to life there are two walls to keep us on the path. One wall is named Arminianism (free will) and the other Calvinism (predestination), and that it does good to bounce off both walls as we go along.

26

How true it is; we need both walls. On the one hand we need to understand the free will of man, and yet on the other, the sovereignty of God. On the one, we need to be firm in our assurance of salvation, and on the other, we need to be warned about being slothful.

Upshot

I would just add, believe like a Calvinist if you like, but behave like an Arminian.

12 Not another set of loopholes...

I have to admit I admire the Amish—hard-working people who lead a relatively simple life. In Indiana and a number of other states, you can drive through their towns, eat at their restaurants and shop in their stores.

I've even seen modern Amish-built recreation vehicles, including campers.

The Amish people cling to their horse-and-buggy lifestyle, free from cell phones, iPads and TVs.

Yet, even they have loopholes.

They can't have a telephone in their homes, and so they walk to the nearest phone booth, often less than a block away.

No electricity—unless you own a business. After all, y'gotta have electricity to make campers.

And run a store.

Or a restaurant.

Safe Sects Sense

What is your loophole? What keeps you from being souled-out to your Lord. What secret love do you hold back from loving God with all you've got??

Upshot

Let's prepare for our hereafter with nothing held back, as the song says, "I wanna get so close to Him that there's no big change on that day that Jesus calls my name!"

13 Why didn't Mom abort me?

I noticed your mom didn't abort you either.
Why not?
A friend who thinks he knows the Bible insists it has nothing about abortion.
My initial response was Psalm 139: 15-16

"My frame was not hidden from you,
when I was being made in secret,
intricately woven in the depths of the earth.
Your eyes saw my unformed substance;
in your book were written, every one of them,
the days that were formed for me
when as yet there was none of them." (ESV)

My friend didn't buy it.
Then one day I was reading in Exodus 21:22-23.
"When men strive together and hit a pregnant woman, so that her children come out, but there is no harm, the one who hit her shall surely be fined, as the woman's husband shall impose on him, and he shall pay as the judges determine. But if there is harm, then you shall pay life for life (ESV)

Safe Sects Sense

"God's laws protecting life included the protection of unborn children. V. 22 refers to a woman giving birth prematurely (i.e., before the baby is fully developed and ready to be born) because of violence done to her....If the mother or child died, then the accused one was guilty of murder. The penalty was to give his or her life (v. 23). In such a case, the unborn child is viewed as a human being and the death of the fetus, or unborn child, is considered murder....This is the only situation in the law where causing someone's death by accident (i.e., manslaughter) called for the death of the offender (cf. Deut. 19:4-10)....God seeks to protect and defend those who are least able to protect themselves, i.e., the unborn." Commentary from *Fire Bible*, p. 125

14 Bad boy or wasted years?

I read a book called *The Bad Boy of Gospel Music*, the story of Calvin Newton.

Food to ponder.

Now, I knew a number of girls that were attracted to bad boys. One or two of those had enduring marriages. The others, not so well.

I didn't qualify as one of those bad boys girls wanted. To put it in polite-company language, I stayed at home by popular demand!

But all have sinned, and so my bad streak manifested itself in other ways. Sneaky ways. I don't remember stealing anything from a store or person, but I'm guilty of not giving 100 percent for the pay I earned.

And I was self-centered.

Calvin Newton got me thinking, however, when he sang a song on the Gaither *Homecoming* series, "Wasted Years."

I've passed up far too many opportunities.

Even so, besides talking to the Lord about it, a quote from Sir Thomas More encouraged me. It's one reason I'm writing this book.

He said, "To buy the time that I before have lost."

That's real hope for you and me. It's never too late.

Pastor Dan Betzer affirmed the idea. His sermon focused on Moses.

Moses tried to weasel out of what God wanted him to do.

Moses the Weasel! And yet, God chose him. God used him mightily, and Moses turned out to be one of the greatest leaders in history.

When Moses protested early-on that he wasn't up to it, Betzer pointed out, God got his attention:

"What is that in your hand?"

A staff.

God used that stick miraculously, starting with an eye-popping demonstration.

God had him throw the staff down and it turned into a snake. He picked it up, and the snake decided it wanted to be a stick again.

What is that in your hand?

What gift, interest or talent has God given you, and how can you use it to help somebody and expand God's kingdom?

What steps can you take today or tomorrow to start?

Safe Sects Sense

Ever notice God uses the least likely person to do his work?

He picked the underdogs.

"God found Gideon in a hole. He found Joseph in a prison. He found Daniel in a lion's den.
He has a curious habit of showing up in the midst of trouble, not the absence. Where the world sees failure, God sees future. Next time you feel unqualified to be used by God remember this, he tends to recruit from the pit, not the pedestal."— Jon Acuff

God didn't pick the eldest or the tallest. He chose the shepherd kid, David.

He chose a prostitute, Rahab

He chose a bunch of cowards like Jonah.

And the 12 disciples.

At a time when a woman's testimony didn't count in court, God chose a woman to announce the Resurrection! If someone were to make up the story, they wouldn't choose a woman!

Another good book, and I credit the author for awakening this idea in me:

God of the Underdogs: When the Odds Are Against You, God Is For You by Matt Keller

Upshot

If God can use and equip those unlikely folks, He can use underdogs like you and me.

15 Fix me, Lord (gently)?

I'm a mess. Friends and family know. But who isn't? No false humility here. After 74 years I have things to work on, and so do you.

I'm not worried about the wrath of God, however. Jesus took my place, took my punishment. It's called mercy (withholding what I deserved) and grace (favor I don't deserve).

People tell me not to pray for patience, because God might respond in a way I don't like.

I'm not concerned—better to put my whole self in the hands of a loving God.

I found a passage in Jeremiah decades ago that I can comfortably pray and apply. I first found it in the *Living Bible*, and now in the *New Living Translation*:

"So correct me, Lord, but **please be gentle**. Do not correct me in anger, for I would die." Jeremiah 10:24 (NLT)

This is something you and I can earnestly pray, trusting God for the outcome.

Apparently C.S. Lewis agrees, as follows.

Safe Sects Sense

Lewis, grieving the death of his wife, Joy:

"What does it matter how this grief of mine evolves or what I do with it? What does it matter how I remember her or whether I remember her at all? None of these alternatives will either ease or aggravate her past anguish.

"Her past anguish. How do I know that all her anguish is past? I never believed before—I thought it immensely improbable—that the faithfulest soul could leap straight into perfection and peace the moment death has rattled in the throat. It would be wishful thinking with a vengeance to take up that belief now. H. was a splendid thing; a soul straight, bright, and tempered like a sword. But not a perfected saint. A sinful woman married to a sinful man; two of God's patients, not yet cured. I know there are not only tears to be dried but stains to be scoured. The sword will be made even brighter.

"But oh God, tenderly, tenderly." --From *A Grief Observed*

16 On the other hand, be careful what you ask for

We can learn much from devoted people in bygone days. After all, they painted, wrote and built great works without the distractions of television or the Internet.

If I needed a whack from a two-by-four, I thought this prayer captured the need:

"Batter my heart, three person'd God; for, you As yet but knocke, breathe, shine, and seeke to mend; That I may rise, and stand, o'erthrow mee, and bend Your force, to breake, blowe, burn and make me new." —John Donne

Oops.

Not long after I started praying this, I suffered two cardiac arrests, both on Friday the 13th of May 2016.

Two weeks later, the medics gave me a stress test. When the results came in, my cardiologist's nurse called and said the doc couldn't understand why my heart stopped—the test showed everything clear.

"I think I know," I responded.

Another cardiologist had prescribed Metoprolol for my atrial fibrillation, usually brought on by too much caffeine. Take two pills. If the A-fib continued for 45 minutes take two more.

Good grief. My heart still flip-flopped after two hours and four pills. Maybe pills five and six would stop it.

Oh, yes, it stopped it, all right. Stopped my heart.

Thank God for quick-thinking emergency medics, CPR, de-fib shock and a jump-start chemical.

Suzanne watched in horror at the gruesome scene in the entry way of our home.

A medic noticed her lips moving.

"Did you say something?"

"I was praying," Suzanne responded.

God answered her prayers, but only after an ambulance ride to the hospital, another cardiac arrest and insertion of a permanent pacemaker.

After that, it only hurt when I coughed, from battering my chest.

"Now I know what it feels like to have a baby," I told Suzanne.

"No you don't!"

Safe Sects Sense

Later, I wrote this:

A year ago today, the lights went out.
My heart went still
Midst the medic's shout;
The villain: a tiny, deadly pill
That didn't cost me a penny,
But I took too many;
Prescribed to make my A-fib drop;
Instead it made my heartbeat stop.
That pill that day was not a hero;
It made my heartbeat go to zero.
Chest battered, electric surge;
Give it up and sing a dirge?
No! Her lips were moving, her spirit calm:
Grace clothed my wife with peaceful balm;
All she knew to do was pray;
His glory now put on display;
Implant pacemaker; life came back;
My goals are now again on track;

Of pills now I am O so wary;
An overdose can be quite scary;
Usurp the doctor, take more often?
Not unless you've bought the coffin;
Now I praise Him, sing and dance,
For some strange reason, a second chance!

Upshot

My friend, Marge, heard that I had a cardiac arrest. She told me later that term meant "death" to her. Perhaps I would have preferred that option had I seen a glimpse of Heaven. I will in time.

In the meantime, you and I should follow doctor's orders

17 Not you, of course

I'm a mess and you're not.
Really?
An agnostic friend says I use Jesus as a crutch.
He's wrong (of course!)
Jesus isn't my crutch. He's my wheelchair. Thanks to Carl for that!
Oh! But my agnostic friend says to offer my own thoughts.
Again, thanks to Carl.
My life comprises the sum total of all of my experiences, teachers, friends, enemies, media, reading…you name it.
If your life is independent of stimulus and input, more power to you!
All have sinned.
My shirt-tail sorta in-laws took me to a Baptist convention. Three Baptist preachers got up and preached their hearts out.
Then the keynote speaker got up.
She blew the others away.
Anne Graham Lotz, Billy's daughter, told about preparing for a seminar. She had a list of 28 sins and wanted to ask how many each had committed.

Suddenly, the Lord spoke and told her she had committed all 28.

She spent the next few days on her knees, making things right with God.

You? Me?

I confessed at one Bible study that I prayed, "Lord, forgive me for selfish pride, backbiting, gossip, mockery, gluttony...."

The leader asked a woman to close in prayer.

"I cannot. I'm under conviction."

Safe Sects Sense

We tend to think of two or three spectacular sins: the preacher who ran off with the piano player; the preacher who trashed his wife after taking up with his boyfriend lover; the preacher who had his hand in the till.

What about the other sins you and I commit?

God have mercy.

Upshot

"Lord, show us our pride, since proud people don't know they're proud." –Mark Vroegop

18 Not so very long ago...

Driving in the Western Washington green paradise, I thought of my Corps of Engineers assistant Leila, who said Seattle was "Heaven to me" after growing up in the Philippines.

Now I see it. This is a small taste of Heaven, compared to those who are desperate for a meal today, those who are tortured or killed because of their faith or those who suffer disease.

There, but for the grace of God, go I.

I don't know why He put me here and now, instead of some (what I think are) awful times and places. But He did. And I want Him to show me what He's working on and to invite me to join Him in that work.

As for Leila, she said her father would never buy a Japanese automobile.

"Why not?"

"They invaded our country during World War II."

On a lighter note, I told Leila I was about to go downtown.

"Would you bring me something from La Petite Boulangerie?"

Shocked and speechless, I finally muttered something.

"Oh, Leila, I don't think that would be appropriate."

"Dave! That's a bakery!"

Safe Sects Sense

A petite woman with a big heart, Leila ultimately practiced forgiveness. She bought a Japanese car.

"Mercy and forgiveness must be free and unmerited to the wrongdoer. If the wrongdoer has to do something to merit it, then it isn't mercy, but forgiveness always comes at a cost to the one granting the forgiveness." —Timothy Keller

Upshot

Leila's big heart produces big results. She's one of the hardest workers I've ever known. I hired her as a GS-3 clerk. Today she's a manager.

19 What's worse—poverty or riches?

I have tried to find the happy medium between my early years as a cheapskate and, later, too many excessive purchases as a spendthrift.

As a tightwad, I missed too many opportunities to travel the world (mostly at government expense near various duty stations).

One time the Air Force provided a career-motivation flight from my base in California to Wright-Patterson AFB, Ohio.

Next-door neighbor Bill had invited me several weeks earlier to spend that weekend with him and his folks in Ohio. But after we landed, Bill forgot all about his invitation.

Unwilling to spend any more money than necessary, I holed up in the bachelor officer quarters and ate hash out of a vending machine. I didn't even visit the world-famous Air Force Museum (I did years later).

It was one of the dullest weekends of my life.

Later the opposite was true when I impulsively bought useless toys that turned out to be a big disappointment.

I'm reminded that as a kid watching Space Patrol (or Cadets), Ralston Cereals offered a spaceship control panel. The picture on the box assured me it was the real thing, with lit gauges and levers.

I mowed lawns with a rusty hand-mower and scrimped until I had enough change and box tops to send in for the shiny console.

When it arrived, I rarely experienced such utter disappointment and despair.

It was dysfunctional, cheap cardboard.

Safe Sects Sense

Remove far from me falsehood and lying; give me neither poverty nor riches; feed me with the food that is needful for me, lest I be full and deny you and say, "Who is the LORD?" or lest I be poor and steal and profane the name of my God. Proverbs 30:8-9 (ESV)

Upshot

"They say when you die your life flashes before your eyes; make it worth the watching!"—cited in the memorial for Brianna Oas Strand

20 I want it *now*

The media have conditioned us to solve any problem in a 30-second commercial. With patience, the problem might go away in 30 minutes—60 max—unless we're watching a movie. Everyone lives happily ever after in two hours.

Delayed gratification went over the side long ago, it seems.

Dad bought two watches. Brother Thom and I would each get one, maybe, but not until the two of us thoroughly cleaned the basement.

Thom had vanished on an overnighter. When would he do his part? I anguished over how to win the watch in the least time, but Thom's absence complicated the desperate situation.

I calculated exactly half the labor in the basement and worked feverishly in order to pass muster and get the watch. Now.

Dad looked at the results, but he remained unconvinced. OK, maybe I claimed the easiest half.

No watch—until Thom got home tomorrow? So unfair!

No, waiting until tomorrow was unacceptable. I dove into Thom's basement territory, cleaning a good portion of his responsibility, as I saw it, to make sure I got the watch. Today.

Nope. Dad said the entire basement must be spotless. That's the deal.

That was the tipping point for me. No way would I let that punk get off free and clear to accept his watch with no work. I wanted him to suffer as I had. It's only fair.

The night and hours before Thom got home seemed like agonizing days or weeks.

Finally, he returned and learned the conditions of the prize. He immediately went to work and finished his portion that I had already done the lion's share.

I had worked six hours on my half. And another two or three hours on his half. He worked less than an hour, and the whole basement shined. Less than one lousy hour.

How fair was that? We both got the same prize for grossly unequal work.

Delayed gratification? OK, ok, I could have waited until Thom arrived to pull his share.

But I wanted that cheap watch so much I could taste it.

Safe Sects Sense

A man hired men at various times of the day but paid each the same at the end of the day, even though one had worked only one hour.

The thief on the Cross made things right with his Savior at the last minute, but he saw Paradise before someone who faithfully served God all her life.

In one way, looking forward to Heaven is delayed gratification. Not really, though. By asking forgiveness, repenting and inviting Christ into my life, I started receiving the benefits here and now—a taste of Heaven.

Upshot

I wouldn't want to live any other way, and living a less-satisfying life with plans to make things right with God on my death bed is just too risky.

21 Or did society's 'progress' make delayed gratification burdensome?

I took a graduate course in human development from Liberty University. The professor outlined expectations of people at various stages, starting from infancy.

He decided to ask his grandmother what expectations society had of adolescents when she was at that age in the early 1900s.

"We didn't have adolescents then. We got married at 14 or 15."

Historians tell us Mary was perhaps as young as 13 at Jesus' birth, and Joseph was around 19.

My mother-in-law had an arranged marriage.

Did society mess up by delaying everything?

At 18, I was least equipped to make monumental decisions about college, career, and least of all, whom should I marry, or even what to look for in a potential wife. I suspect most young people are likewise clueless.

Too often we make goofy choices with consequences. Accordingly, when I needed money the most for a growing family, I had least, and much later, when I needed less, I had most.

Safe Sects Sense

A famous general granted an interview.

"General, to what do you attribute your success?"

"Two words: good decisions."

"Yes, but General, how does one learn to make good decisions?"

"One word: experience."

"Of course, General, but how does one develop essential experience?"

"Two words: bad decisions."

Upshot

On the other hand, perhaps that's part of life—learning by struggling through limited provisions, scant options and unwise choices.

22 Welcome news despite indecision

I have so many interests that my mind splatters in every direction, easily distracted with myriad options. I'm often frustrated by too many enticing alternatives.

I nominated Patricia Graesser to enroll in a year-long on-the-job course as management intern, now called leadership development.

She came back from class one day and told me that I exemplified a management style they had studied. Really? With my indecision and all?

"You're a participatory manager!"

Who knew?

Often reluctant to make a choice, I often asked my staff for input and recommendations.

One time I needed to send a staff member to a Corps of Engineers project at a dusty, isolated place. I detested the thought of going myself. I'll send Rita.

No, that would be too cruel. Better go myself. I don't wanna. Send Rita. How unkind. Go myself.

I tossed and turned all night. The next morning, I told Rita to go.

Another office mate piped up.

"How come I never get to go?"

Safe Sects Sense

Others relish adventures we'd rather decline. And because of the gifts God gave us, the reverse may be true.

Upshot

The late, great Paul Harvey told of the hardships members of the Salvation Army endure. He suggested it was because of a sturdy pair of shoes they're issued.

It must be those shoes, he insisted.

"We all want to go where they are going without having been where they have been."

23 Broadcast deception

I served evening shifts as an announcer to fulfill one of my assignments as a broadcast student at the University of Washington.

I wrote "continuity copy," promos I read between tapes of stuffed-shirt lectures.

Dad asked me what time I would work my shift at KUOW-FM, and I told him 6-8 p.m.

When I got home, Dad said he listened during that time.

"Did you broadcast during that shift?"

"Sure, Dad, did you listen?"

"I didn't hear you on that station."

"Dad, I was using my big-boy voice!"

In television and radio broadcast you will find fake voices, fake names, and pretty faces.

I had a face for radio.

A fellow instructor at the Defense Information School, Dick Cassin, had once performed as a technical sergeant, serving as a DJ overseas with Armed Forces Radio.

He made up a character, Airman Basic Rod Carlisle. If Dick spilled coffee, he'd blame Airman Basic Rod Carlisle.

Dick would even page the imaginary airman at the base theater. Everyone thought the poor, klutzy Airman Basic Rod Carlisle actually lived somewhere on base.

Years later, Dick, now a civilian, would select outstanding broadcast students at our school. He presented them with a prestigious certificate.

In bold letters, the certificate honored the student as a recipient of "The Rod Carlisle School of Broadcasting and Storm Door Company Award."

Safe Sects Sense

We find numerous deceivers in the Bible. I've been guilty in the past—"white lies" or worse. I'd rather have my epitaph find me straight-up trustworthy as someone whose goal was to be more like Jesus. I suspect you would as well.

"He committed no sin, neither was deceit found in his mouth." 1 Peter 2:22 (ESV)

24 Heard anything more profound in all the universe?

My dear wife said two things not only unheard by me in all of history, but unheard by most all throughout the history of the universe:

(1) Though she dearly loved her daddy and mother, she said their loss was nothing compared to the thought of losing me; and

(2) St. Paul in Romans 9:3 said he'd be willing to go to Hell to save his kinsmen. Blows my mind!!!!!!!! I asked my wife: "Would YOU be willing to go to Hell to save your offspring?"

Said she: "I would."

Can you think of anything more stunning? Wracking my brain, I cannot.

Safe Sects Sense

I know you're having so much fun. Jesus offers more. A man I know joined a faith-based, live-in substance-abuse recovery group to get his family off his back. He determined not to stay the course. He would hustle them.

"Jesus outhustled me," he later confessed.

Upshot

He started his own successful faith-based recovery group, totally dependent on God.

25 The creator-frog

A young man studied tadpoles in a pond near his college dorm. Somehow the tadpoles would disappear and frogs entered the scene.

How did that happen?

He concluded that frogs created the world, using tadpoles as building blocks for everything that existed.

Unfortunately, the young man's college existed in a totalitarian nation, and all creator theories violated the law.

Nevertheless, word traveled fast among students and peasants that the young man had discovered the origin of life.

He knew it was a farce, but he rather enjoyed the notoriety.

Unfortunately, his fame presented a clear-and-present danger to him. The authorities had decided he must undergo torture and an agonizing death for dreaming up the creator-frog.

When the police arrested him, he said he had top-secret information and needed to see a Supreme Magistrate.

Fearing reprisal for obstructing the reporting of classified information, the police captain arranged a swift hearing—behind closed doors, of course.

Immediately after the hearing, the young man was released. The Supreme Magistrate had given him one chance to recant. Knowing he made up the fantasy, he willingly discarded—recanted—the fictional theory.

He was free.

Safe Sects Sense

No one in his or her right mind has ever in history submitted to a tortuous death knowing the story for which he was charged was untrue.

It's the same with the Resurrection of Jesus. Timid cowards, followers of Jesus, scattered during Jesus' trial, but after he arose from the grave, these same men, now transformed, became bold and confidently proclaimed the Resurrection—even to each one's terrible death, never recanting.

They knew it was true.

Upshot

Dr. Gary Habermas, among others, has presented convincing evidence for the Resurrection that even many skeptics accept. He debates the doubters all over the country.

"I can get them to the Resurrection," he insists.

Hamermas describes in detail the many circumstances of the excruciating death, the empty tomb, initial disciples' despair-turned-emboldened, change to Sunday worship, Paul's conversion, Jesus' brother James' change of heart after experiencing appearances of the risen Christ, eyewitness accounts, enemy attestation and secular affirmation.

There are 18 non-Christian sources affirming the historical Jesus.

There is far better evidence for Jesus than for Alexander the Great.

However, one of the most convincing to me: No male fictional writer in that culture would use women to announce the Resurrection; as mentioned elsewhere, a woman's testimony was invalid in court, and so it must have happened just like they said.

26 Lying is OK?

Evangelicals raised me. As an adult I initially questioned much of what my parents taught me. But after scholarly research (rather than pop culture and the Internet), I found there's not much of an alternative truth-bearing choice.

Let's look at one example, Islam. There is a technique the Soviets used—lying is good if it advances the cause of the state—a principle charged against the DoD spinmeisters like me during the Vietnam War. However, I was never asked to lie.

And yet, this principle is a doctrine of Islam, called *Taqiyya* (cover-up, disguise—alternate spellings *Takiya, Takiyah*). Islam sanctions lying to or deceiving others to advance the cause of Islam or to preserve its "good" name. As for Islam, "It permits the suspension, as the need arises, of almost any or all religious requirements, or its doctrines—including a total denial of faith— when fearing threat, injury or compulsion of any kind in a non-Muslim society, or even in a Muslim Society." (Sam Soloman, citing AL Zamakhshari and Fakharadin A'razi)

Some question whether it is a *bona fide* "doctrine." And yet, one can show in their own backgrounds "doctrines" that have little backing in scripture.

I would ask, "Is taqiyya a term actually used in Islam? Yes.

45

Is such deception actually practiced in Islam? Yes.

The words of Jesus permit no such deception under any circumstances. Love is the operative word. As I've said elsewhere, the Resurrection is a smoking gun as nailed down by the scholarly work of Dr. Gary Habermas in *The Historical Jesus*. And this truth has a bonus—a very long-lasting and joyful relationship with the Founder!.

Safe Sects Sense

Not surprisingly, I find it easy to reject the teachings of Islam, and that includes the abuse and subjugation of women, including the mutilation of genitalia, sex traffic and forced marriages, often of young girls. An increasing number of Muslims are turning to Christ through testimony and even dreams.

Upshot

A young Muslim daughter was paraded before cameras. She was proudly wearing a simulated suicide vest, eager to come of age and use it to destroy infidels.

My question: Why doesn't she ask, "Daddy, Grandpa, if wearing and using a suicide vest is so noble, why haven't you warn one and used it long ago?"

27 God evens the score regarding gender

Timothy Keller has opened my eyes about a number of things. You would do well to look him up.

For one thing, in his *Prodigal God* he faults the elder brother more than the wayward son. In fact, it's the elder brother who ends up wayward by his self-righteously looking down his nose at his returning brother.

Keller says there are too many high-and-mighty elder brothers (and sisters) in church. I've been there, and you have, too.

The older I get, the more undeserving I discern about myself, save but the Blood of Jesus.

How about you?

Another glorious discovery, thanks to Keller:

"Many take offense at using the masculine word 'sons' to refer to all Christians, male and female. Some would prefer to translate Galatians 3:26: "You are all children of God" (as the NIV 2011 does). But if we are too quick to correct the biblical language, we miss the revolutionary (and radically egalitarian) nature of what Paul is saying. In most ancient cultures, daughters could not inherit property. Therefore, 'son' meant 'legal heir,' which was a status forbidden to women. But the gospel tells us we are all sons of God in Christ. We are all heirs. Similarly, the Bible describes all Christians together, including men, as the 'bride of Christ' (Revelation 21:2). God is evenhanded in His gender-specific metaphors. Men are part of His Son's bride; and women are His sons, His heirs. If we don't let Paul call Christian women 'sons of God,' we miss how radical and wonderful a claim this is."—Timothy Keller

Safe Sects Sense

A text without context can be a pretext for a proof text.

28 Finally, an apt word

Lacking muscle and motor skills, I needed a coach.

When Dan Koser and I worked at King's Garden in the student-work program for 440 hours during the summer, only the two or possibly three of us stayed in the boys' dormitory.

In the center of the dorm, workers had built a gym. With no TV, Dan and I spent hours shooting baskets and lifting weights. Dan playfully would "beat me up," explaining he was toughening me for the upcoming football season. He had talked me into trying out for the team.

Dan's toughening program inflicted pain, but not as much as at church that fall.

"Fall" perfectly defined Dan's ultimate pain-inducing act.

Interbay Covenant Church had a long flight of stairs leading to the basement classrooms and fellowship hall. Without notice, Dan pushed me down the stairs, hoping somehow to perhaps desensitize me to agony.

I laughed it off and tried not to show by my expressions how much it hurt.

Not until decades later did I find the perfect quotation to describe his act:

"Some people are like Slinkies; they're not very interesting until you push them down the stairs!"

Safe Sects Sense

But I discipline [or buffet] my body and keep it under control, lest after preaching to others I myself should be disqualified. 1 Corinthians 9:27 (ESV)

A person finds joy in giving an apt reply—and how good is a timely word! Proverbs 15:23 (NIV)

29 Others more beautiful by far

Of beauty I'm not a star;
There are others more beautiful by far;
But my face, I don't mind it,
For I am behind it;
It's the people in front that I jar.—Unknown

I convinced my lifelong buddy Dan to consider enrolling at King's and sign up for the summer work-study program. His folks brought him to school and I showed them around the campus, including the gym enclosed by the boys' dorm. Dan, ever the athlete, begged his folks, and they consented to enroll him.

That year, the lettermen—K-Club—convinced Dwight Nyquist, Wheaton College football legend whose dad had been our pastor at Interbay Covenant Church, to become head coach at King's. Dan eagerly inquired about turning out for football the next fall.

When summer arrived, Dan and I shared a room in the dorm and whistled in harmony while we washed dishes, pots and pans. During the day, Alice Emerson, a cook, would bake cinnamon rolls and we'd grab a couple while they were still warm, slather them with butter and devour them.

On one assignment, I was the only guy on a clean-up project. Several girl-student workers approached me. Interesting, I thought. But they had no interest in me.

"Who's your handsome friend?"

I told them more than I wanted to about Dan, and it wasn't long before I played matchmaker, arranging a walking date with the tall blonde. Initially, my only dates were vicarious!

Not long thereafter, however, someone introduced me to a girl, and we became a foursome—no wheels, just walking or sitting, mostly.

We were on a beach—Echo Lake?—and Dan stole a kiss. Awkward. I hadn't the slightest skills when it came to smooching, but that afternoon I experienced my first kiss.

Apparently, the administration got nervous about having 22 girls in their dorm and two boys in ours. We had dates every night, and so King's hired Becky Judd's older sister Jan and her husband Jon as recreation directors. That summer was most memorable—softball games, seats at the Aqua Follies on Green Lake in Seattle and a number of fun outings.

Having no wheels until after graduation limited outings to double-dating. When driver Loren Postma broke up with a girl, it pretty meant I did, too. No transportation.

With minimal motor skills causing me to walk oddly and with memories of grade-school boys laughing at my running style, I entered college thinking that finding a wife was next to hopeless.

Now I had a 1948 Desoto, but it wasn't cool like my buddies' cars, and it didn't attract any female attention.

I tried to date a girl as a freshman, but she soon ended the quest without telling me why.

Somehow I ended up marrying beauty, after learning that such things as personality, kindness, talent and commitment should enter into the equation, and that works both ways.

Safe Sects Sense

The person who had more influence on the world, creation, history and the universe—Jesus—wasn't a handsome man, despite how some paintings portray him.

For he grew up before him like a young plant, and like a root out of dry ground; he had no form or majesty that we should look at him, and no beauty that we should desire him. Isaiah 53:2 (NIV)

Upshot

If you're depending on outward good looks as a foundation for a solid, enduring relationship, your priorities are upside down. Yes, homeliness isn't at the top of the list of what we find attractive, but beauty must be more than skin-deep.

How many times have we seen Miss Sparkle hitch her wagon to Mr. Universe, only to discover he's a jerk who mistreats her or runs off.

Then, we notice that Sparkle falls madly in love with a geek who treats her like a princess.

And they live happily ever after.

30 Sometimes it pays to mumble

Our junior class adviser, Mrs. Rood, asked me to write a senior prophecy for the graduating upper class, for presentation at a banquet.

I wrote it as a two-person simulated broadcast, thinking I would play the role of one broadcaster and a girl would take the other part.

Our planning committee recommended the name of a girl to Mrs. Rood, and she approved.

"She can work with Dave and practice together," a committee member suggested.

Thinking I was out of earshot, Mrs. Rood responded, "Not Dave. He mumbles."

It hurt. The committee talked her into letting me perform, and ever since, I usually try to enunciate very clearly.

But not always.

Late for an appointment with the base commander years later, a major came into my office and wanted my opinion on a publicity matter.

"OK, but can you make it snappy?" Not the kind of thing a first lieutenant should say to a major.

He abruptly stated his business, and then ambushed me outside. He gave me the tongue-lashing I well deserved.

Irritated, I mumbled, "Yes I know I should bow and scrape to you guys."

Thankfully, he didn't hear the mumble.

Sometime later, when I taught journalism to all five armed services, I thought a written mumble might have some utility.

Penalizing otherwise good writing for spelling errors, I conceived a new key for the typewriter—a carefully designed strikeover key. One wouldn't know if you intended an "o," "e," "a" or "i."

It would appear as a well-meaning smudge.

Safe Sects Sense

Beloved, do not believe every spirit, but test the spirits to see whether they are from God, because many false prophets have gone out into the world. 1 John 4:1 (NIV)

Upshot

I told a young girl who noticed smoke coming out my '71 Volvo's exhaust pipe that I needed to have the valves ground.

"Oh, I know what they are—a, e, i, o and u!"

Spelling is a challenge, even with spell-checker. The best writing advice Dan Koser said he got from me: "If you're not sure how to write or spell it correctly, back up and write around it."

31 Misspell the general's name
& your knickers will be aflame

It's so important to spell someone's name properly that when I taught journalism, I failed students for incorrect spelling of a name.

Sure enough, the Air National Guard newspaper at Fairchild committed the deadly sin. General Hague replaced General Braig.

In bold letters, the headline announced the change of command for Haig and Braig.

Dan Koser was a partner of a utilities consultant firm in San Diego.

He maintains a list of misspellings of his name by salesmen and clients who took valuable time and energy to write him.

"Dear Mr., uh, Crozier, Koshier, Kozer, whatever…"

Safe Sects Sense

Slack habits and sloppy work are as bad as vandalism. Proverbs 18:9 (MSG)

32 Call me 'Possum

In South Korea in 1971, I mostly stayed in my room when I didn't participate in chapel activities.

My goal: to read the Bible, cover-to-cover, for the first time. I tried to read the King James Version Pastor that Pastor Ted Nyquist gave me when I graduated from confirmation class.

Just before bedtime, I'd head for the communal shower, walking past dorm-mates playing Hearts. Not knowing these guys, having recently arrived, I kept mum.

One day the guys poured water under my door. They tried to "smoke" me out. They succeeded. I joined in their card game.

Charlie, the Munitions Squadron commander, had given each man in the dorm an animal nickname. He called me "'Possum," and said he picked it because he thought all this time I had hung by my tail from the ceiling in my room.

My friend Gene Neudigate's dad could neither read nor write, although he was good with figures and managed the Eli Lilly apple orchard, selling apples and making change.

"C'mon, Son, get in the car. We gotta get home and watch Arthur Gospree!"

Gene laughed.

"Dad, it's not Arthur Gospree. It's Godfrey."

Irritated, his dad had a quick reply.

"Who do you think you are, Boy, a 'fessor?"

Gene's dad insisted he had attended 'Possum College in Frog Town, Kentucky, just north of Slickaway.

I believe him. Those were real towns.

When the University of Kentucky played the University of Louisville in Indianapolis for the NCAA basketball tournament, Gene fretted.

"The restaurants will have to order extra 'possum!"

Safe Sects Sense

"In the last time there will be mockers, following after their own ungodly lusts." Jude 1:18 (NASB)

However… Sarah then said, "God has given me cause to laugh, and all who hear of it will laugh with me." Genesis 21:6

The story of Abraham, Sarah and Isaac is familiar to most Christians. God promised to give Abraham and Sarah a son, but they did not believe him because Sarah was very old and no longer fertile. Yet God has a sense of humor, and Sarah became pregnant and gave birth to Isaac. In fact, the name Isaac means "He laughs," in Hebrew. God indeed does have a sense of humor, as most of us know.

One of the greatest compliments I hear my wife tell people: "He keeps me laughing."

Upshot

One person in my men's group tells me he learns a lot from me, and adds, "If you would just knock off the silliness and be serious."

Another brother tells me he enjoys hearing from me because "you brighten it up with humor."

Who's right?

A third brother says, "Just be yourself."

33 Delivered child named after ambulance driver

I loved Conrad Green's adult Sunday School Prime Timers class. This bunch began in their mid-30s and now have more than doubled their ages, but they refuse to "graduate" into the old-folks' Olympians class.

Conrad's parents owned a mortuary and ambulance service, and the family lived above the business.

One day a woman in labor called for the ambulance and Conrad's dad picked her up. Half-way to the hospital, the woman screamed, "The baby's coming!"

The ambulance pulled over, and Conrad's dad delivered the baby.

The baby's mother, overjoyed, named the child after the ambulance driver-deliverer.

"I often wonder whatever happened to that baby," Conrad told us. "That child must be middle-aged by now."

He concluded, "It's not often you come across a girl named Chester!"

Safe Sects Sense

Name your child with care. Biblical names, for example, can inspire a child to live up to his or her moniker.

Upshot

My friend suffered with the name Shirley Eugene. Born about the time as Shirley Temple, the name could easily describe a boy or girl until she made it a a popular name for a girl.

"Don't call me Shirley," Gene often complains, paraphrasing Psalm 23. "Shirley, Goodness and Mercy are sheepdogs, and they shall follow me all the days of my life."

34 Speaking of delivered...

Someone brought us a stray cat when we lived in Heidelberg, Germany. We named her "Heidi."

We lived in an old German townhouse, complete with one of those toilet- or drinking-fountain-looking contraptions that bubbles up water for hygiene. It's called a bidet, pronounced bid-DAY.

One day I noticed a strange deposit.

I told Suzanne, "The cat left a calling card in the bidet. It looks like a hunk of liver."

She responded, "HALLELUJAH! She's been de*liver*ed!"

Safe Sects Sense

"Delivered" has many meanings, especially expressed by a Pentecostal. And we all want to know we've been delivered—from demonic influence, from sickness, from oppression, stress, heartache, loneliness, toxic people, toxic substance and false teaching.

35 Speaking of demonic influence...

While we lived in Germany, our church denomination asked me to lead a Friday Night Fellowship for American soldiers and civilian workers. Volunteer "lay pastors" who led various denominational groups registered with the Army chaplain, and when the chaplain's office received a call from someone of our denomination, the specialist referred the caller to a lay pastor.

One time, when I wasn't home, a woman who claimed to be a member of our denomination called our home.

Suzanne answered.

The woman said her name was Trixie, and she knew that Bruce Springsteen had planned to come to Germany. Trixie wanted to come to the Friday Night Fellowship so that I could lay hands on her in prayer.

Prayer for what?

She explained that she and Bruce had been married when they lived in Heaven, and the prayer would enable them to be married on earth.

She said that she and Bruce had sat on the Throne of God, and that God allowed them to write the Song of Solomon!

"Sometimes we wore white robes in Heaven, but at other times, we walked around naked."

Shocked, Suzanne didn't know how to respond and quickly ended the conversation, suggesting perhaps I could respond later.

When I heard the outlandish story, I sought the advice of an Army chaplain of our denomination in another part of Germany. What should I do if she showed up on Friday night?

"Go ahead and pray for her. She obviously needs prayer, and it can't hurt!"

Fortunately or unfortunately, she never showed up.

Safe Sects Sense

Pray anyway. We did.

Upshot

We heard that Trixie approached another church. No better place to go when you need help, besides going to God directly.

36 666—the answer stared me in the face

Another caller in Germany from our denomination—we never saw her in the fellowship—wanted me to take immediate action.

"The extension to call the Army Hospital is 666. You need to have them change that."

At a loss for what to say, I asked her to call in a couple days after I looked into it.

What do I do now?

I prayed for divine guidance and opened my Bible. After thumbing through a few passages, my eyes landed on the page number: 666.

Thank you, Lord, for that answer.

The woman never called back, but I was ready:

"Sister, do you have your Bible ready? Please turn to page 666. Now, what should we do about that page—tear it out?"

Safe Sects Sense

Thank God for answers to prayer, but consider diplomacy. Perhaps I could have worded it better!

37 Dedicate my life to Jesus with a 'faggot'?

One of the most powerful and meaningful services at Bible camp included a campfire. Beside the fire, staff had gathered a pile of small hunks of wood from the beach.

You could step up in front of the campers, pick up a hunk of wood and throw it on the fire symbolizing you were offering your life as a sacrifice to Jesus. You declared to all within earshot that you would live your life completely for the Lord from now to eternity.

Many participants' voices faltered. Some campers fought back tears.

That little hunk of sacrificial wood had a name: faggot. The profound service you just participated in was called a faggot service.

Why don't you hear of such a dedication service at camp anymore?

Safe Sects Sense

Language changes over time. It's important to be sensitive to changing meanings. Some changes make sense. Some don't.

Even language usage in the Bible changes over time. That's why we have the *New* King James Version and other translations, though the Hebrew and Greek remain the same.

The Los Angeles Times banned the word "normal."

"Why did they ban 'normal,'" my intern asked.

"I suppose they think everyone is gifted."

"Then wouldn't it be *normal* for everyone to be gifted?!"

Upshot

Overheard: "KJV, thou and thee, behold and lo, I'll never let go!"

38 Shaken and calmed by eternity

Once again a lightning bolt of truth reconfirmed to me God's existence and His love and adoption of me personally. I'll put it in the form of a parable:

God thought of me before the beginning of time. He decided to create a unique creature whose name, He decided, would be David (meaning "Beloved") Harris. At first He had to decide whether to make me a slug, an ant, a snake, a giraffe – or what?

Then, in Genesis, He made a breathtaking statement: Let *us* make [a] *man* in *our* image. So, right off the bat, He revealed the Godhead as plural. He didn't mean "us" as the heavenly hosts – I was not made in the image of an angel. I don't have wings.

"Us" clearly meant Father, Son and Holy Spirit (confirmed in the New Testament). Then He/They had to decide to place me – when? In Ethiopia, on an anthill, in 4,000 B.C.? No, He had a purpose for a baby boy to be born in 1944 A.D. It was a special purpose to inform people of "Christian hedonism" – finding ultimate joy and exhilarating pleasure in their Savior.

That child was to be a "joy boy." He was to grow up to be a Glad Dad and a Happy Pappy. But the process of creating this child was mind-bogglingly complex. There was one egg of the Christian mother – and millions of sperm from the godly father. If the wrong sperm united with that one egg, the resulting child would have been Larry or LaVerne.

So, by human standards the odds of that one sperm connecting with that one egg were staggering. And yet, it was an easy thing for God. And God knew that child would be useless but for some adversity. He saw to it that child experienced what it was like to be poor, sick, weak and like Jesus, "…he had no form or majesty that we should look at him, and no beauty that we should desire him."

God, for the child's ultimate benefit, made one leg shorter than the other and allowed him to develop some motor skills later than his peers. Those experiences, along with being chosen last on every ball team, caused him later to know compassion for those with similar struggles – exactly as God said.

Later in life, shaken by the concept of eternity, he finally realized the "impossible odds" of his being chosen—chosen—to live and thrive in two millennia, two centuries, in the most blessed nation in the history of the world.

If God could pull that off, then eternity is easily mastered. An immaterial God—Three in One— created a material universe and somehow chose David for here and now, even showing him how he readily could, in big and small ways, join the Creator in contributing David's life, David's blood, and David's fortune to those who struggle.

The now-grown child cannot take credit. It is God's doing. And in realizing all this, David, at last is speechless and, awed, marvels at the immensity and monumental order of the whole decision process that led to the endless creation, world without end.

Safe Sects Sense

C.S. Lewis helped me to somewhat grasp the concept of timeless eternity. Lewis compared God to a playwright.

Writing a play, the author describes a woman pouring herself a cup of tea.

Suddenly, the playwright gets up from his work and tends to other errands for two weeks. Then, he sits down and resumes his story. The woman takes her first sip of tea, which is still hot, even though 14 days of time had passed in another realm.

God has no time restraints.

Upshot

Someone else compared eternity to a perfectly formed ring. It has no seams. It has no beginning or end. Wedding rings symbolize a bond that never ends.

39 Nuttin' you gotta do. Nuttin'. Period.

I simply couldn't agree with a lot of what a consultant said when he came to the Army Corps of Engineers.

Co-opting New Age (this kind of touchy-feely course can no longer, by law, invade the federal workforce), he wanted us to use "affirmations."

Just keep repeating, "I am the richest man in the county." Someday it would come true.

As Dad said, "Bosh!" Hogwash.

But the consultant said something that made the Safe Sects Hit Parade:

"Take out a piece of paper and write down everything you need to do today."

I diligently wrote down about 10 items. So did the others.

"Wrong. You don't have to do any of those things. You choose to do them. You didn't have to get up today. You didn't have to come to work. You chose to."

Of course, shortly after that, something called me away from work. I called a subordinate, who heard the consultant, and asked her to take my place at the boring budget meeting.

Her response: "I choose not to."

I reasoned with her that she had the freedom of choice, and consequences accompanied her choice.

She complied.

Safe Sects Sense

Live as people who are free, not using your freedom as a cover-up for evil, but living as servants of God. 1 Peter 2:16 (ESV)

Upshot

For which of you, desiring to build a tower, does not first sit down and count the cost, whether he has enough to complete it? Luke 14:28 (ESV)

40 The top 10 things I learned from my dog

10. My dog strives to stay on the straight and narrow way—to go through the straight and narrow gate. Even though she's trim enough to go through the narrowest gate, there are some places she is unable to go and needs my help. She's old. She needs help getting up into the bed or car. The broad way leads to destruction. I once had a dog who bolted onto the broad highway and was destroyed. Not this dog. My dog is also "narrow"-minded – she tolerates other people in the good sense of tolerance, but she doesn't waste her time accepting or excusing their sinful or harmful ways.

Safe Sects Sense

A purposeful life requires a long-range vision. The greater success: live a focused life fixed on the narrow way, trusting Jesus for 80 years, which has far greater reward for eternity than performing one moment gloriously. "Strive to enter through the narrow gate, for many, I say to you, will seek to enter and will not be able."—Luke 13: 24

9. My dog is free to run because my dog knows her boundaries and lives to please her master. My dog strives to keep herself free from distractions and wrongdoing.

Safe Sects Sense

Christ offers freedom from the imprisonment of sin— freedom not to indulge self, but to serve others. "Then you will know the truth, and the truth will set you free." John 8:32

8. My dog is fearless, because she loves greatly and knows she is greatly loved. I love this tiny, elderly dog so much that when it became painful for her to go on walks with us, I started wearing a dog-carrier. She felt safe from big dogs and cars.

Safe Sects Sense

To whom do you and I need to demonstrate more love in order to provide a warm feeling of a secure place in our world? "Perfect love drives out fear." 1 John 4:18

7. My dog demonstrates a kind of love that is clear, deliberate, real and obvious without even uttering a word (although, yes, she also uses her tongue).

Safe Sects Sense

I often wondered how I might exhibit the command to love my God with all my heart, soul mind and strength, and my neighbor as myself, until I heard a preacher on the radio say, "Most of the time when the Bible mentions love, it's talking about commitment. Wow! Commitment is something I can do! "Dear children, let us not love with words or tongue but with actions and in truth." 1 John 3:18

6. My dog sticks closer than a brother. My dog follows me all over the house.

Safe Sects Sense

Let's ask ourselves, "Am I the kind of friend that laughs when my friend laughs and cries when he or she cries, or am I a fair-weather friend?"

"The man of many friends [a friend of all the world] will prove himself a bad friend, but there is a friend who sticks closer than a brother." Proverbs 18:24 (Amplified Bible)

5. My dog focuses on me as her Audience of One. Just as I should pay no mind to praise or scorn from men but act for my Audience of One.

Safe Sects Sense

An Audience of One – "I have been helped by an illustration that I often remember and meditate on. The story is that of an accomplished young pianist making his concert debut at Carnegie Hall. His playing was magnificent and after he departed from the stage the audience erupted in cheers. The kindly stage manager urged the young virtuoso to go out for his encore. But the young man refused.

The older man replied: 'Look out through the curtains. They love you! Go take an encore!' The pianist answered: 'Do you see the one old man in the balcony on the left?' The stage manager peered out and answered that he did see him. 'That man is seated. I will not give an encore until he stands and cheers.'

Exasperated, the stage manager said, 'Only one man is not standing, and you will not take an encore?'

At this, the pianist replied, 'You see, that old man is my piano teacher. Only when he stands will I go take an encore.'"—Richard D. Phillips

"Beware of practicing your righteousness before other people in order to be seen by them, for then you will have no reward from your Father who is in Heaven." Matthew 6:1 (ESV)

4. My dog teaches me how to be a fool for Christ, as Paul describes us. Paul is talking about Christians, but the dogs of the world could be saying this:

Safe Sects Sense

"It seems to me that God has put us who bear his Message on stage in a theater in which no one wants to buy a ticket. We're something everyone stands around and stares at, like an accident in the street. We're the Messiah's misfits [or fools]. You might be sure of yourselves, but we live in the midst of frailties and uncertainties. You might be well-thought-of by others, but we're mostly kicked around. Much of the time we don't have enough to eat, we wear patched and threadbare clothes, we get doors slammed in our faces… When they call us names,…we say, "God bless you." When they spread rumors about us, we put in a good word for them. We're treated like garbage, potato peelings from the culture's kitchen. And it's not getting any better." I Cor 4:9-13 (MSG)

3. My dog has forgiven me seventy times seven.

Safe Sects Sense

It's hard to forgive—until we remember how very much we've been forgiven. "And Jesus prayed, Father, forgive them, for they know not what they do." Luke 23:34

"Blessed is the nation whose God is the LORD, the people he chose for his inheritance."- Psalm 33:12

2. My dog is a patriot, prepared to defend me. A patriot is someone who vigorously supports his or her country and is prepared to defend it against enemies or detractors.

Safe Sects Sense

"Even though I walk through the darkest valley, I will fear no evil, for you are with me." Psalm 23:4 (NIV)

Finally, the **number 1** thing I learned from my dog:

Listen to what Greg Laurie says: In our culture, if you were to say of someone, "He's a real Superman!" it's a sure bet everybody would know what you meant.

In the same way, when John the Baptist said of Jesus, "Behold! The Lamb of God who takes away the sin of the world," his meaning was not lost on his listeners.

Every Jew immediately understood what John meant by the Lamb of God. The law taught them to atone for their sins by bringing an animal sacrifice, likely a lamb. A priest would take the animal, kill it, then symbolically take the sin of the worshiper and place it on the animal.

Everyone knew what it was to see lambs slain to atone for their sins. Jews would think back to the Passover when God told them to take a lamb, slay it, and put the blood on their doorposts.

Many Jewish homes would take this lamb into the house as a pet. Can you imagine having to sacrifice your pet dog?

But they intentionally did it [became close to the pet] so that real affection would develop, thus heightening the sense of loss when the animal was finally killed. They would feel the pain of it and realize the pain God felt when they sinned against Him....There is an interesting progression in the commands about the Passover lamb in Exodus 12. First God said take "a" lamb. Then "the" lamb. Then "your" lamb.

So the **number 1** thing: My dog endeared herself to me, and told us she was ready to die at age 15. She was old, mostly deaf and her eyes were weak. And when I think of her even now, I think of God's pet Lamb whom He gave up to die for me.

Safe Sects Sense

"Behold, the Lamb of God, who takes away the sin of the world!" John 1:29 (ESV)

Upshot

I want to be a narrow-minded, free, fearless, focused fool for the Audience of One.

41 'But if not'—no one knows what it means anymore

During German air raids over England in World War II, signs all over the nation proclaimed a simple message of never-say-die determination.

"But if not."

Everyone—man, woman and child—knew what those three words meant. The cry of defiance came from Daniel 3:18—**But if not**, let it be known to you, O king, that we do not serve your gods, nor will we worship the gold image which you have set up. (NKJV)

Originally, three young Jewish men, Shadrach, Meshach, and Abed-Nego, had decided they would refuse to bow down to the idolatrous image the Babylonian king had set up. The young men knew a fiery furnace awaited them if they disobeyed.

Their faith assured them that God could easily rescue them…"but if not," they would willingly go to their tortuous death rather than to recant their allegiance solely to the God of Israel.

God ultimately preserved them in the midst of the red-hot furnace, so that their hair was unsinged and not even the smell of smoke came from their clothes.

The English people knew their God could keep them from defeat by the Germans.

"But if not…."

No matter which way the war turned—victory or defeat—the people would continue to serve and worship God.

And God gave them victory.

Safe Sects Sense

Coward administrators in schools fear so much about getting sued by one or two atheists that school children display ignorance of basic concepts of the Bible, such as a common phrase: Pilate "washing his hands" of any blame for condemning Christ.

Upshot

Sadly, if you displayed "But if not" in a million places in the United States today, how many would have a clue to what those words meant.

42 Misplaced identity

A wise, old friend was talking to his troubled grandson who was in and out of juvenile facilities. "I'M THE ANTICHRIST," the grandson proudly proclaimed.

The wise response: "The Antichrist will be a brilliant man to sway billions of people. You're too dumb to be the Antichrist!"

End of grandson's identity crisis.

Most of the trouble in the world happens because of identities gone awry. You need only one identity: follower of Christ. More? Faithful, loving spouse-parent-sibling-son-daughter. Even more? Hard-working, contributing, civil-speaking American.

Safe Sects Sense

"But Dave, you've failed in some of those." Thank God for redemption and not a performance-based standard. And thank God for those who still love an undeserving pilgrim, including my long-suffering, glorified, intercessor Savior, my patient wife and family.

For by grace you have been saved through faith. And this is not your own doing; it is the gift of God, not a result of works, so that no one may boast. Ephesians 2:8-9—see below for the next verse.

Upshot

Dallas Willard reminds us that God favors effort, but **not** earning. Where do good works fit in? They are post-salvation actions designed to make us more and more like Christ. It's called sanctification.

For we are his workmanship, created in Christ Jesus for good works, which God prepared beforehand, that we should walk in them. Ephesians 2:10

43 Tarry, Lord

Mom Helen McMillin experienced a transformed life when she found Jesus, who cleaned up her language and delivered her from cigarettes.

With a grade-school education, she diligently read a chapter of the Bible every day.

She had experienced a troubled life early on—an arranged marriage to an abusive man and a divorce. But then she married the love of her life, my wife's daddy, who died at 70.

She subsequently married Harold, and the two of them helped build a church. Sadly, Harold died in her arms at Burger Chef.

Her fourth husband, Jim, loved her but troubled her by impulsive spending. Then he died of heart trouble.

Now she just wanted to go home to Jesus, and that was her wish for more than a decade.

Her family couldn't understand why Jesus didn't take Mom home. Two heart attacks and a paralyzing stroke diminished her quality of life in a nursing home.

Startled that she had survived so many husbands, a family friend thought he knew why she lingered on.

"Helen had four husbands in Heaven petitioning the Throne, saying, 'Tarry, Lord, tarry!'"

My wife replied with one of her quick retorts.

"I don't think the first one made it."

Safe Sects Sense

A prominent television preacher, asked whatever happened to Adam, responded, "Adam's in Hell."

How does he know?

D. James Kennedy told of a scoundrel in early America who embarrassed his nation here and abroad with his constant immoral behavior.

However, on his death bed, the scoundrel wrote in the margins of his books, "Christ forgive me. Christ save me."

Upshot

Kennedy said he had read hundreds of death-bed confessions. Don't ever count someone out. And don't wait that long yourself. You may not have a clear-minded chance in the last moment.

44 Brilliant means of chewing on delicious morsels amid truth and error

A good friend put me onto an excellent application for navigating biblical principles. I looked up the folks that put it out, and they proudly proclaim themselves as part of a sect that embraces false doctrine.

I pointed this out to my friend, and he knew that. But the program itself focuses only on the Bible and presents no bias or error in the references.

Safe Sects Sense

"Count me as one who eats the meat and spits out the bones," he said.

Upshot

This has enhanced my freedom among the peril of conflicting opinions. I know one prominent preacher who has enlightened me on certain truths, but I know he's dead wrong on others. Rather than toss out the baby with the bath water, I carefully glean the good fruit, careful not to ingest the bad.

Yes, count me as one who eats the meat and spits out the bones.

45 An unforgettable trigger to remember diplomacy

Coach Dwight Nyquist taught us high-school boys about diplomacy.

"Remember," he said, "there's more than one way to say what's on your mind."

I'll never forget his example.

"You could say, 'Woman your face would stop a clock!' or a better way to say the same thing is, 'Baby, when I look at you, time stands still!'"

Safe Sects Sense

A soft answer turns away wrath, but a harsh word stirs up anger. Proverbs 15:1 (ESV)

46 Cold, lukewarm or hot?

Try drawing a horizontal line on a board, write "hot" at one end and "cold at the other, turn the board around so others can't see it and ask classmates privately to put a mark where they think their own spiritual temperature is.

Most likely, the majority will put their marks near the middle.

Then, you pull a fast one and quote the verse, "So, because you are lukewarm, and neither hot nor cold, I will spit you out of my mouth," says Jesus in Revelation 3:16 (ESV)

You'd admonish the class not to be cold, and not lukewarm, but to commit their lives to heat up their relationship with Jesus through prayer, reading the Bible, serving and giving.

But wait!

Dad gave a delightful sermon as a guest speaker at Interbay Covenant Church in 1988. He said that in Revelation, Jesus wrote a love letter. Dad gave me a whole, new perspective.

He looked up the Greek for "cold," and described it as something like a "cold, refreshing drink of water."

Aha!

So, rather than lukewarm, I should seek opportunities to refresh people like a cold beverage.

What about hot?

When the devoted missionary baptized me in Korea, he warned me not to attend one of his denomination's "stone-cold churches" when I returned to America.

"Unless," he admonished me, "you're willing to light a fire under them!"

Safe Sects Sense

Likewise, two people lying close together can keep each other warm. But how can one be warm alone? Ecclesiastes 4:11

Upshot

The heroic ship captain Ernest Shackleton masterminded the legendary rescue of his shipmates after the sinking of the *Endurance* in Antarctica. Despite bone-chilling months of misery and danger, Shackleton returned home with every sailor. Not one died. The men kept warm at night by combining their body warmth and sleeping in a circle with feet pointed to the center and touching the legs of the others.

My maternal grandfather worked for this great leader before the voyage. Shackleton instilled a sense of adventure in my grandfather, who wrote a series of boys' adventure books about the Yukon and Northwest Territories.

47 Disasters—the only way I could go was up

God has blessed me in my media spokesman career with a trail of disasters.

A number of my assignments came as a result of failure by my predecessors.

The Air Force terminated one Air Force captain caught naked in a downtown elevator.

My first assignment arose because the wing commander, base commander and public affairs officer lost their jobs over a local incident involving young Civil Air Patrol cadets who went on a joy ride in an Air Force truck wearing stolen flight uniforms. The story metastasized into a national incident called "The crying colonel caper."

You can read about it my earlier book, *Treasure Trove in Passing Vessels*, available (cheap) on Amazon's Kindle.

Safe Sects Sense

March on in humility and thankfulness for the gifts God gives you when your work follows failure.

Upshot

Expectations are low and your every effort will shine in triumph. Take care, however, to avoid feelings of superiority. People tend to compare your work with others, but don't fall into that trap.

We do not dare to classify or compare ourselves with some who commend themselves. When they measure themselves by themselves and compare themselves with themselves, they are not wise. 2 Corinthians 10:12 (NIV)

Do not consider yourself to be superior. Romans 11:8a (NIV)

48 Boycott everything?

Our pastor years ago suggested that the congregation boycott any store that sells pornography. Presumably that meant hard or soft porn in magazines. I'm told men don't need to go to a store for such today—the internet offers one's fill. This boycott was pre-internet.

We wanted to comply, until we learned we might have to avoid going virtually anywhere in town.

We couldn't go to the grocery store.

We couldn't go to the drugstore.

We couldn't go to the Navy commissary.

We couldn't go to the Navy Exchange.

Since then, concerned pressure groups have warned us against shopping at Home Depot and Target because of their contributions to anti-Christian organizations.

My question: if we go to Lowe's or an alternative store, how do we know they're not somehow contributing to seedy evil-doers?

On the other hand, secularists asked us to boycott Chic Fil-A because of its Christian values.

It backfired. Now cars line up around the block.

Safe Sects Sense

Stephen the Martyr looked up at the point of his death and saw Jesus standing. Doesn't scripture say Jesus now sits on the throne at the right hand of his Father?

Turns out that Jesus stands up for us when we stand up for him!

Upshot

One McDonald's McCafe, seeing record crowds, put the following on their billboard:

"How about boycotting *us*?"

49 Can you scale the high bar of this marriage test?

One of the members of our Men's Roundtable offered advice that revolutionized his marriage. He said his wife often would ask him to do something for her and like a good husband, or so he thought, he resolved to do it as soon as the game was over or he finished reading the paper.

Then, challenged to do what he could to put a little "oomph" in his marriage, he stumbled on a new approach. Whenever his wife asked his to do anything, he immediately would stop what he was doing and execute his wife's task pronto.

He didn't practice this just once. He kept responding immediately.

He reported that somehow it did wonders for his marriage.

Safe Sects Sense

Dear children, let's not merely say that we love each other; let us show the truth by our actions. 1 John 3:18 (NLT)

Upshot

There's action, and there's self-reflection. Once again, it doesn't hurt to keep asking myself, "Would I want to be married to me?" Action can have startling results.

50 Is it a sin to drink?

I know a retired master chief who never drank alcohol in the Navy, even before he was a Christian. So one day, knowing a typical sailor's love for coffee, I offered him a cup.

He politely declined, saying he's a gulper, not a sipper.

I've read many accounts for and against Christians drinking alcohol.

Bill Gothard taught that what we practice in moderation, our children will excuse in excess. I've seen it happen.

Someone said that alcohol doesn't bring others—or me—closer to the Lord when I'm drinking, but further away.

Have you heard anyone say that Jack and Coke made them feel closer to God?

Alcohol makes it much harder for someone to exhibit the biblical attribute of self-control.

A friend whose dad made alcoholic drinks went to seminary to be a pastor. The school prohibited alcohol on campus and advocated an alcohol-free lifestyle.

"But what about Boaz? Didn't he enjoy wine after a hard day in the field?" My friend put the question to his seminary professor.

"That's true, Boaz did enjoy his wine. But like so many other things, once the devil gets hold of it, it can become sin."

Safe Sects Sense

In prayerfully considering both sides of the question, I recommend getting a copy of the *Fire Bible*, Donald C. Stamps, General Editor, and published by Hendrickson Publishers Marketing, LLC. You can find it through Christian book distributors and Amazon.

The commentary gives rationale why many references to wine in the Bible can (but not always) refer to fresh, sweet grape juice. However, J. Vernon McGee taught that sweet wine had an extra dose of alcohol.

Deuteronomy 14 talks about bringing one's tithe to worship in the place that God chooses, but if it is too far away to carry the tithe, the worshiper may turn it into money and buy "whatever you desire—oxen or sheep or wine or strong drink, whatever your appetite craves. And you shall eat there before the Lord your God and rejoice, you and your household." (ESV)

The commentary suggests that the drink was not alcoholic, since the command to worship included children and priests (who were to abstain from intoxicating beverages in such rituals), and in order to distinguish between the holy and profane.

Upshot

While most study Bibles take a strong Calvinist view, the *Fire Bible* considers the free-will viewpoint, as well as the position that gifts of the Spirit are for today, not ending when the apostles died. McGee teaches that under grace we aren't under the rules of men, but on the other hand, walking in the Spirit means not to do anything that would dampen one's relationship with the Lord—or offend a weaker brother. Whatever we eat or drink, we are to do it all to the glory of God, His Word tells us.

Man's rules or God's? One young man complained to his counselor that he wasn't allowed to play a full game of basketball on Sunday. But he was allowed to shoot hoops. The counselor challenged him, asking whether that was man's interpretation or God's.

"Is it all right to play a game of h-o-r-s-e?"

More on "rules" in Chapter 53. Whatever you prayerfully decide about eating or drinking to the glory of God, review Chapter 27 and let's ask ourselves if we're the elder brother in the story of the prodigal son. Do we look down our noses or backbite people who behave differently than we do?

51 Better get used to those folks

Suzanne and I like cruising with Princess, because those ships schedule what they call "unhosted Bible studies," which means ship's officers don't lead them.

Someone may ask, "What's your favorite Bible verse," and often a lively discussion ensues to everyone's delight.

Sometimes, however, a person will take over and dominate the discussion—again and again and again over many days.

On one cruise, I emailed my sister Kathy.

"The leaders present sound scriptural applications, but some of their worship habits seem rather strange. I'm not sure I can stay with this bunch."

Always wise, Kathy opened my eyes.

"Hang in there," she replied. "Get used to them.

"You may be living next door to them in Heaven."

Safe Sects Sense

If possible, so far as it depends on you, live peaceably with all. Romans 12:8 (ESV)

Upshot

Suzanne's stepdad, "Grandpa Jim," drove 18-wheel trucks for a living. One day in church he asked for prayer, because his dispatcher made it hard to get along.

His family suggested that Jim pray for the dispatcher every day.

After a short time, Grandpa reported what a positive change had come over the dispatcher.

We're not sure if God changed the dispatcher's attitude.

Or Grandpa's.

Or both.

52 Symbolism or substance?

How about faith in action?

When I awoke from a cardiac arrest and insertion of a pacemaker, Suzanne told me that my friend, Dan, had boarded a plane from San Diego to come up and see me.

Since I had known Dan since fourth grade, I would have appreciated knowing he had faith for my recovery.

He wanted to demonstrate his faith. He put wings on it. He acted on his faith.

Dan initially went to the ICU, but thankfully, they had released me.

So Dan visited me in our home. His presence, coming from a long distance, contributed immensely to my healing.

Safe Sects Sense

So you see, faith by itself isn't enough. Unless it produces good deeds, it is dead and useless. James 2:17 (NLT)

Upshot

I knew how and where to find this verse, because I had heard a Bible teacher speaking far more powerfully than I had expected. I realized he was reciting Proverbs. He inspired me to memorize. But I didn't think I could handle the whole book of Proverbs.

Someone had told me that the book of James took the role of the proverbs of the New Testament. And so I determined to memorize it, and I did. The whole book rolled off my tongue.

Now the bad news: if you don't keep reviewing what you memorize, it leaks out. However, if someone quotes a passage in James, I know where they got it.

John Piper said his father died of Alzheimer's, and John could see himself potentially going that way as well. But, he said, memories of teenage foolishness still resided in his brain, and he didn't want that coming out in his sunset years. Instead he saturated his heart and mind with scripture, hoping that would come out instead.

And then he recited Philippians, with great expression, from memory.

53 Human rules or God's?

A number of young people get turned off to the overwhelming spiritual benefits of the Gospel, not because of God's guidelines, but because modern-day Pharisees add their own rules to what the Bible says.

In younger days, the church asked me to represent youth at a district conference. Someone got up and presented proposed rules for Bible quiz teams. No sleeveless dresses.

Oddly, the proposal included no rules for boys.

Before the vote, I conferred with my young pastor and proposed that the delegates vote instead on an amendment to suggest quiz-team participants dress and act according to prayerful guidance from the Holy Spirit, and leave it at that.

The young pastor agreed, but he said that tradition would rise up against such an amendment. However, he presented it to a fellow young pastor, and the delegates voted as I had suggested.

Astonished, my pastor told me the amendment lost by just one vote! Progress.

Safe Sects Sense

If with Christ you died to the elemental spirits of the world, why, as if you were still alive in the world, do you submit to regulations—"Do not handle, Do not taste, Do not touch" (referring to things that all perish as they are used)—according to human precepts and teachings? These have indeed an appearance of wisdom in promoting self-made religion and asceticism and severity to the body, but they are of no value in stopping the indulgence of the flesh. Colossians 2:20-23 (ESV)

Upshot

It's important to read the whole message of the Bible in context. Otherwise, people tend to overdo things at one extreme or the other.

Among folks profoundly affected by a sermon or revival, changes in behavior result. But when they try to force those behavior changes on people who weren't present and impacted by the move of the Spirit, rebellion can result.

It's important to lovingly communicate—with grace and truth—the genuine, contextual, scriptural reasons behind any behavior demands, carefully explaining the rich spiritual benefits that accompany such devotion.

54 The 3 birds sitting on me

Wanting to know all the options before I make a decision, I often think that three advisor birds perch on my shoulders and head.

One is the Dove of the Holy Spirit. One is a devilish sort of bird. I'm not sure who the bird is on top of my head, but I taught my journalism students to look for more than two sides of a story. Another point of view needs to come to light, and that third bird whispers an alternative viewpoint.

The devilish bird's duty is accuser. He tells me I'm a terrible guy, undeserving of Heaven. The Dove tells me that Jesus paid for my sins with his blood on Calvary, and no matter what the accuser says, I'm Heaven-bound.

The bird on top of my head tells me I have mixed motives and even quotes scripture to me that my heart is "deceitfully wicked" and I cannot trust my thoughts or heartfelt feelings.

Example: I played organ at several churches, and the Dove told me such service, carried out in humility, honored God. The devilish bird told me I performed with pride. The accuser tempted me to look around to see who was listening, that I had conflicting motives.

At the Men's Roundtable, one brother told me he learned a lot from me and he enjoyed the lessons laced with humor.

Another brother expressed his appreciation for my input, if I could somehow curtail the lighthearted quips.

A third brother told me just to be myself.

Safe Sects Sense

The Bible settles the argument regarding my eternal home: The Spirit himself bears witness with our spirit that we are children of God. Romans 8:16 (ESV)

And yet the three birds try to challenge each other about that.

I asked my friend, Gene, how he came to know without a doubt that his salvation was settled.

"After I invited Jesus into my life, God changed my desires," he said. Instead of the usual worldly activities, I could hardly wait to get home after work, change my clothes and go to camp meeting!"

That's right. The Holy Spirit changed my desires, as well. Now, instead of the shallow things I used to read, I love to go deep into God's Word and dig out the precious gems therein. I thoroughly enjoy studying what godly men and women have discovered about how those truths apply to them.

Upshot

A dear brother told me he delayed asking Jesus into his life, thinking how much he'd have to give up. But when the evidence became clearer and he committed his life to Christ, he marveled that what he gained so far exceeded what little he gave up.

55 Am I walking, standing or sitting

So, on the way to work, this feller I heard about walks past a strange place. What kind of place is it, anyhow?

The next day, he walks past the same place.

"I think I know what that place is. It's a brothel!"

The third day he is about to pass the brothel, and he stops and stands and ponders the whole scene.

Finally, he not only walks to the place and stands, but he goes in and sits down.

That's how it is with temptation. We walk past it. Then we stand and look. Then we go in and sit down.

If we have the Holy Spirit, he gives us the power to keep on walking.

Or better yet, running.

Safe Sects Sense

Blessed is the man who **walks** not in the counsel of the wicked, nor **stands** in the way of sinners, nor **sits** in the seat of scoffers. Psalm 1:1 (ESV)

Upshot

No temptation has overtaken you that is not common to man. God is faithful, and he will not let you be tempted beyond your ability, but with the temptation he will also provide the way of escape, that you may be able to endure it. 1 Corinthians 10:13

56 Basketball humorist

Gene Neudigate's days as a high-scoring basketball guard at Indianapolis' Broad Ripple High School makes him a legendary name even in his eighties.

Renowned author Dan Wakefield wrote about Gene and his family. In one of Dan's books he recalled walking by the Neudigate home as a young man and seeing "Jesus Saves" in the window.

Decades later he wrote nostalgically of shooting baskets with Gene as boys and Gene's going on to play as one of the top-scorers in Indianapolis for Broad Ripple High School.

Gene said his coach never swore. Instead the coach would stop practice with a lesson, signaled by "Son, son…."

One day, the coach, particularly exasperated, told his team, "Boys, I'm going to deflate this basketball and give it to the art department to make it into a purse. That way, it will be more effective than what you're doing with it!"

Safe Sects Sense

Fathers, do not exasperate your children; instead, bring them up in the training and instruction of the Lord. Ephesians 6:4 (NIV)

Upshot

Gene's wife has multiple sclerosis, and Gene, being the ultimate neatnik, happily does most of the housework.

He lovingly teases about his trim wife Colette and says she asks for a doggie bag at a restaurant, puts the leftovers into the refrigerator at home and never finishes it.

One day, Gene decided to clean out the refrigerator.

"Colette, what is this pudding?"

I wonder if she actually answered or if he stretched the truth.

"That's not pudding; that's corn on the cob!"

Wonder no more.

57 Real presence?

I'm changing the names to protect the innocent.

Ralph, an evolving Evangelical, visits his brother Justine every year in Toledo.

Justine kept the Catholic faith the two grew up with. Ralph, however, troubled by how little his former Catholic parishioners knew about their own faith, accepted the challenge of a friend to look into the assurance of salvation offered by the Gospel of Grace.

Now, years later, he accompanies Justine to Mass once a year and asks a lot of questions, hoping to win Justine to faith alone by grace alone in Christ alone.

"What's in the chalice?"

"It's the Blood of Christ."

Justine, a recovering alcoholic, accepts the bread of Communion as the Body of Christ, but refuses the any wine-dipped mode.

"If it's no longer wine and now blood, why can't you drink it?"

Ralph doesn't press the issue in hopes of keeping peace in the family.

After studying extensively about what the communion elements are and represent, I've concluded the following (with a surprise ending):

* Communion is symbolic of Christ's death.

* Communion is more than a mere ritual, but is a deep commitment and relationship with Christ and his Bride, the Church.

* When Jesus talked about eating his body and drinking his blood in John 6, he hadn't yet introduced communion. Jesus celebrated communion—the Lord's Supper—later in the upper room in conjunction with the Passover meal.

* In John 6:51, Jesus said, I am the living bread that came down from Heaven. *Whoever eats this bread will live forever.* This bread is my flesh, which I will give for the life of the world." We can all agree that **not** just anyone who partakes of communion will live forever. Repeat, not.

* When Jews ate the Passover meal, they ate the Bread of Affliction, which is symbolic, and not actual affliction they were now experiencing.

* I accept the biblical evidence that Jesus' glorified, physical body—his human nature—means that though he retains also his divine nature, he willingly, physically sits at the right hand of the Father and doesn't materialize in more than one place at a time. Thus, his body doesn't physically materialize in the mass, particularly in the many celebrations of the mass.

* A number of well-documented positions exist on what the bread and wine become or represent, including consubstantiation, or Christ "with" the elements.

* Transubstantiation (turning bread and wine into the actual body and blood of Christ) wasn't proclaimed until 1215 by Pope Innocent III.

* Christ is present in the Lord's Supper by sending his Holy Spirit, bringing his divine, real, spiritual presence.

* Someone asked R.C. Sproul in a seminar I attended: My relatives claim to have a genuine salvation experience the same as we believe, but they continue to attend the Roman Catholic church and practice their rituals. Will this keep them out of Heaven? Sproul responded to this effect (paraphrased): Maybe. While there may be a number of genuine, born-again believers in the Catholic church, I believe that the Roman church doesn't preach the biblical Gospel, that is, salvation is by faith alone by grace alone in Christ alone. They preach a gospel of works and they offer no assurance to a devout believer of assurance of salvation.

* MISUNDERSTANDING: DO CATHOLICS TEACH THAT CHRIST IS "PHYSICALLY PRESENT" IN THE MASS?

*When describing Jesus Christ in the Eucharist, Catholics will say that the Lord is "really," "truly," "wholly," "continuously," or "substantially" present, **but not "physically."** To say that Jesus is "physically" present is to suggest that he is present "locally" (as he is now in Heaven at the right hand of the Father). The eucharistic presence of Christ, although understood as no less real, is a sacramental presence in the (transubstantiated) host. From the Catechism of the Catholic Church:*

1413 By the consecration the transubstantiation of the bread and wine into the Body and Blood of Christ is brought about. Under the consecrated species of bread and wine Christ himself, living and glorious, is present in a true, real, and substantial manner: his Body and his Blood, with his soul and his divinity (cf. Council of Trent: DS 1640; 1651).

Castaldo, Christopher A. *Talking with Catholics about the Gospel: A Guide for Evangelicals* (pp. 128-129). Zondervan. Kindle Edition.

Safe Sects Sense

Every day the priests stand and do their religious service. Again and again they offer the same sacrifices, which can never take away sins. But Christ offered only one sacrifice for sins, and that sacrifice is good for all time. Then he sat down at the right side of God. And now Christ waits there for his enemies to be put under his power. With one sacrifice Christ made his people perfect forever. They are the ones who are being made holy. Hebrews 10:11-14 (ERV)

Upshot

As promised at the beginning of this book, here is the secret of the universe and everything holy (adapted from an audio statement by Dallas Willard): Does believing all the correct doctrines get you to Heaven, as important as they are? No. Even the devil knows all the correct doctrines. **What gets you to Heaven is sincerely, genuinely and consistently trusting Jesus to empower you to live your life as he would live it if he were you!** See Galatians 2:20.

58 What does it mean to trust Jesus?

Trusting Jesus means to give yourself up to him, turning from sin, relying on him and determining to live in him day by day and moment by moment, confessing our failures to him, fellowshipping with fellow believers and seeking his purposes through prayer and studying his Word, the Bible.

Read the book of 1 John. You'll be relieved to know that this trust grows gradually and that, though we will stumble at times, God is eager to forgive us as we confess our wrongdoing and turn from it. This process is called "sanctification," and it is a lifetime journey to become more and more like Jesus. And yet, we'll never achieve perfection until we see him face-to-face in Glory.

Safe Sects Sense

How do we stay on that journey consistently to become more like Christ? Spend time with him and his Word in a daily, sincere quest. And without faith it is impossible to please God, because anyone who comes to him must believe that he exists and that he rewards those who earnestly seek him. Hebrews 11:6 (NIV)

Upshot

What happens if I get off track? I heard a teacher explain it this way: If you ride a bike and fall off part way to your destination, what do you do—walk it back to where you started? No. You get back on the bike and continue the journey.

59 More love for Jesus? I was troubled about that

I know: And he said to him, "You shall love the Lord your God with all your heart and with all your soul and with all your mind." Matthew 22:37 (ESV)

When I read how very much God loves me, I feel so inadequate saying I love him back. And yet, one translation says to love him "with all your passion" (MSG) or another says, with all you've got."

I feel like I come up short so often.

But a black preacher on the radio provided some help. He said that most of the time, when the Bible talks about love, it's talking about commitment.

Commit with passion, with all I've got.

Yes! I can commit (and that includes action).

Lord, I love you. "More love to Thee O Christ; More love to Thee!"

Safe Sects Sense

"If you love me, keep my commandments." John 14:15 (ESV); "If you love me, show it by doing what I've told you. (MSG)

Upshot

You and I can make that lifetime commitment today.

60 Godly woman 'preaches' without words

Dee Koser, my lifelong friend's mother, consistently displayed love, patience, service, humor, grace and good humor—the joke was often on herself. I felt so welcome in her home that I ran there as soon as I could on Christmas morning to experience her joyful zest for life.

Dee taught Sunday School and served wherever the needs arose. She faithfully attended the Sunday morning services after Sunday School.

One day—through Bible reading or a prompting of the Holy Spirit—she felt that she needed to resign from her Sunday School duties in order to stay home and cook a grand breakfast for her unchurched husband Con. Con regarded breakfast as his favorite meal of the day.

The couple spent leisurely Sunday morning hours over coffee, bacon, eggs and toast, to Con's delight.

Then, promptly at 10:45, Dee kissed Con good-bye and headed to church for the 11 o'clock service.

This joyful routine continued for several weeks and months.

One Sunday, as Dee prepared to leave for church after breakfast, Con stopped her.

"Can I go with you?"

Con became a regular attender, and one Sunday morning, at the invitation of the pastor, Con knelt at the front and gave his life to Jesus.

Safe Sects Sense

Wives, in the same way submit yourselves to your own husbands so that, if any of them do not believe the word, they may be won over without words by the behavior of their wives, when they see the purity and reverence of your lives. 1 Peter 3:1-2 (NIV)

Upshot

Schedule regular quiet times to listen to that "still small voice" of God prompting us to do little things that matter according to his purposes so that our faithfulness will result in God's bigger assignments that have a greater and greater impact for God's Kingdom.

61 What if she's lying?

As a supervisor at the Army Corps of Engineers, I attended a required class on sexual harassment.

The instructor showed a video of a dirty-old-man boss who, behind closed doors, tried to seduce his secretary, who reported him to human resources.

After the video I asked, "What if she lied?"

The instructor replied that in such a case, if the boss claimed she was lying, human resources would investigate to see if the boss exhibited a behavioral pattern.

"Put a glass door on my office," I demanded.

Soon a workman installed the glass door, and over my 40-plus-year career, I never had such a charge against me.

Hiring-practice complaint? Yes. That was another matter. But my co-workers helped me provide documentation that the complaint had no substance. I had offered the complainant a job and she wrote to my staff declining the position.

Safe Sects Sense

"You shall not bear false witness against your neighbor." Exodus 20:16 (ESV)

"Whatever you do, work at it with all your heart, as working for the Lord, not for human masters, since you know that you will receive an inheritance from the Lord as a reward. It is the Lord Christ you are serving." Colossians 3:23-24

Upshot

"You may be sure that your sin will find you out." Numbers 32:23 (NIV)

62 Speaking of sin finding you out...

When son Michael attended junior high school, he asked his mom if he could attend a certain movie with his friends.

"I'll research it to make sure it's a wholesome film," she responded.

Later Suzanne told Michael we'd approve his seeing the movie, "but only that movie, and none other."

Three hours after he departed for the show with his buddies, our front door slowly opened. Michael stealthily moved toward his room without a word.

His mom spotted him. "You didn't see the movie you told me you wanted to see, did you?"

Startled, Michael responded, "How did you know?"

"Be sure your sins will find you out," she calmly replied.

Safe Sects Sense

Now there are diversities of gifts, but the same Spirit…to another discerning of spirits. 1 Corinthians 12:4, 10

Upshot

Many times the still, small voice of God revealing a secret can get one's attention in such a profound way as to keep one on the straight and narrow for life.

63 Discovered too late? Live and learn from my (or others') mistakes

I noticed a persistent chill in the Indianapolis house I had purchased near 56th Street in the mid-seventies.

I knew I needed to take action when I put my hand over a kitchen electrical outlet and felt a cold breeze blowing through.

Checking out several insulation companies, I found a new company that had introduced a gooey foam that could be squirted between studs. It would harden and seal up any intruding drafts, the salesman said.

The good news: no damage to walls or ceilings. Workmen would drill through the mortar of the brick exterior and fill the gaps.

They got to work, and I delighted at this modern way to solve the problem, until BOOM! A workman drilled all the way through the brick and dry wall into the bedroom!

No big deal. He patched the wall and repainted.

Later, a company executives told me they lost money on the deal—part of the learning curve of a new venture—because they used far more foam than they had estimated. Nevertheless, they assured me, the house would be toasty warm the following winter.

Not so. Winter came again, and the cold breeze still blew through the electrical outlet.

I don't recall the outcome. If my memory serves me, the company had found no solution to the never-fill foam and went belly-up.

The following summer I sold the house, and I moved out.

Just to make sure I hadn't left any tools in the crawl space, I climbed under the house with a trouble-light. Sure enough, I shed light on trouble. The gaps between the studs on the walls had no flooring underneath.

The crawl space had filled up with foam.

Safe Sects Sense

I have hired a number of interns over the years at the Army Corps of Engineers.

"Don't be afraid of making mistakes, lots of them.

"Then, learn from your mistakes so that you don't repeat them."

64 Two words altered my life

Having failed advanced calculus at Seattle Pacific College, I knew I should have majored in journalism all along, but this college offered only introductory courses and writing opportunities on the *Falcon*, the college newspaper.

I knew I'd have to transfer to the University of Washington in two years to complete my chosen field of study. I obtained a course catalog from the "U" and took only courses at SPC that would fulfill the "U's" graduation requirements.

Upon arriving at the university two years later, I was shocked that their new catalog had changed the requirements. I could not fulfill the new curriculum before my draft deferment expired in June 1966.

I drafted an angry letter to the faculty's academic standards committee.

"I demand…" that the committee allow me to fulfill the standards according to the earlier catalog.

I decided to run it by my faculty advisor, a calm, white-haired professor who pondered my belligerent draft while smoking a pipe.

"Son," his fatherly advice began, "I suggest you rewrite this letter and substitute two words—*respectfully request.*"

He convinced me; I revised my tirade with the two magic words and submitted it.

The committee approved, and I graduated on time.

Safe Sects Sense

A word fitly spoken is like apples of gold in a setting of silver. Proverbs 25:11 (ESV)

Upshot

I successfully have used those words virtually every time I had a formal request for the last 50-plus years. Often old goats have wisdom under their snowy locks.

65 German delights and one of the 3 Stooges

Working as a civilian public affairs officer for the U.S. Army in Europe turned out as one of our greatest memories as a family. We looked forward to eating croissants from the neighborhood bakery for breakfast and tackling the delicious schnitzels.

I must warn you, though, that cakes in German bakeries look rich and sweet, but the Germans use less sugar, and so the cakes may be better for you, but they can disappoint the American sweet tooth.

Soon after arriving, I attended the Friday Night Fellowship in our military community of Heidelberg. I learned that the leader, Bob

Dyche, and his family would soon return to America. He nominated me as his replacement.

To qualify as a lay preacher, the Assemblies of God had to interview me to determine my spiritual suitability.

"Tell me about you and your wife," he began.

"Well, I'm the creative one in the family and my wife is the one with the common sense."

He thought a moment and said, "We're glad to have your wife in Europe with us."

I learned how difficult it is to try to serve as a part-time pastor. Over the next year-and-a-half, the group re-sized from about 30 to about, well, five.

I had just served a federal assignment at Fort Harrison, Indiana, as assistant professor of journalism, teaching all five branches of the military, a job I loved and where I learned to speak publicly.

Pastoring involves much more, and I fell short.

With no Air Force Reserve unit in Heidelberg, I fulfilled my annual requirements by serving as an Air Force Academy admissions officer. I interviewed young military family members who had indicated a desire to apply.

One benefit: the Heidelberg Officers Club had an unsurpassed brunch buffet every Sunday for a mere $5. I took the family almost every Sunday. Some weeks later, I learned the delectable meals were available only for club members. Civilian federal employees were to pay $11 a month.

About the time I discovered the requirement, a letter came from the Academy offering associate membership in their club for $2 a month. Membership meant access to any military club in the world.

I eagerly accepted. Of course, the Academy expected my appearance to be impeccable, wearing my uniform to every interview of a prospective cadet.

One time the parents of a young man called me to arrange an interview. They needed to meet with me right away.

Problem: my hair was too long, with no time to get a haircut.

I enlisted the help of Suzanne. She reluctantly complied and grabbed the clippers.

"Oops!"

"What's the matter?" I asked.

"I cut your sideburn too high. Now you look like Moe of the Three Stooges!"

Now I know why people kept staring at me whenever we went out to eat for the next three weeks.

Safe Sects Sense

May he equip you with all you need for doing his will. May he produce in you, through the power of Jesus Christ, every good thing that is pleasing to him. All glory to him forever and ever! Amen. Hebrews 13:21

People look at the outward appearance, but the Lord looks at the heart. 1 Samuel 16:7

66 Square peg in a round hole

OK. It all makes sense now. My mechanical ineptitude became obvious as early as first grade, if not before.

Every day I walked about four blocks to the main street to catch a city bus to school. One morning, Mom gave me a business-size envelope to mail in the box on the utility pole. I could barely reach the narrow pull-down door to the slot, and try as I might, the envelope kept hitting an obstacle inside the slot. I couldn't get the letter to drop.

Finally, a kindly woman walked up and offered to help. She simply turned the envelop 90 degrees and deposited it horizontally. I had attempted to force it vertically.

A simple thing, you may think—a test easily failed by a 6-year-old.

But somehow my genes just didn't understand spatial orientation.

Before that, I frequently put my shoes on the wrong feet. Exasperated, Mom drew an "X" on each insole.

No help. I continued to put my shoes on wrong.

Communication is essential, I learned during my ultimate career. Mom never told me what her markings meant.

Safe Sects Sense

In the public affairs career, we wrote stories that became news releases, command briefings or internal news articles. As professional communicators, we thought we did well.

We found out, however, that our communications between public affairs co-workers often failed.

I finally offered one edict that markedly improved the situation. "Read your own stuff," I pleaded.

Upshot

When we read our own emails and texts before hitting the send button, the world perks up and our days go quite a bit better, improving relationships, which is what God was up to all along.

67 Identity theft?

Shortly after Suzanne and I got married, and she became Suzanne K. Harris, she opened an account at the Fort Harrison bank. When she got her paycheck, she asked me to deposit it.

Those were the days before computers.

The paycheck didn't show up when she got her statement several weeks later. She asked me to check with the bank.

I explained the situation to the teller, and she disappeared for several minutes.

"Is your wife Susan K. Harris?"

"Well, no. That was my ex-wife's name."

Oops.

Suzanne finally got credit for the amount.

Safe Sects Sense

Judah, Jacob's boy, thought his disguised daughter-in-law was a prostitute, leading to an embarrassing predicament in Genesis 35. But even after his sin, God put him in the genealogy of Christ, likely to demonstrate that we, all of whom are sinners, can find redemption only through Jesus, the Way, the Truth and the Life.

Upshot

One feller says, "Do you s'pose we'll be a-recognizin' each other in Heaven?"

"Not if'n we don't a-start a-recognizin' each other here on earth."

68 God sightings—his hand upon my life

I should be dead right now.

In 1973, stationed at Fairchild Air Force Base, Wash., near Spokane, I drove many times to nearby Medical Lake. I paid little heed to a weather-beaten railroad cross-bar sign. The paint had faded so much one could barely read what it said. I raced across the rusty tracks without even looking. I didn't even think about it.

Then one day, merrily driving my usual route, I heard an ear-splitting whistle.

I missed getting hit by the train by 5 feet.

Many times since, I didn't see a car or truck coming.

I had a collateral duty at Fairchild as courier, carrying top-secret pouches as a passenger on a C-47. On one occasion I had delivered a pouch to Malmstrom Air Force Base, Mont.

Shortly after takeoff in the prop plane, headed home, the plane suddenly made a nose dive back to base. As we taxied, several fire engines raced alongside.

"What's wrong? I asked the pilot.

"Prop wouldn't feather," meaning it wouldn't reverse as a braking technique.

I thought I was toast.

I found myself too often in the wrong place at the wrong time, or lost in a tough neighborhood, or doing or saying something stupid to a stranger who could have punched or shot my lights out.

Walking in the pre-dawn downtown Seattle on the way to the bus stop on a work day, I saw an old pickup truck run a red light, endangering the ferry pedestrians trying to cross the street.

Unthinking, I slapped the bed of the truck to alert the driver he nearly hit us. I resumed a brisk pace, as if I were unaware.

A couple toughs in the truck stopped and started yelling.

I survived.

Many other close-calls, involving chainsaws, table saws, bike rides down cliffs...

God has a purpose for my life—and yours, and he sends his guardian angels.

Safe Sects Sense

I've often said the worst thing that could happen to me is to have my life detailed in the Bible for all of history to see.

Fortunately, I noticed many of the Bible characters acted as dumb as I have on occasion, and grace happened.

God protected people from their stupid mistakes—people like Jacob, Peter and Paul—and made something unexpectedly profound out of their lives.

Upshot

God-sized challenges require God-sized creative remedies.

69 Eternal adventure

God bless folks with such a passion for sharing their life-transforming experience with Jesus that they organize national or global campaigns.

I'm no good going door-to-door trying to introduce people to Jesus.

I think it goes back to when Dad encouraged me to sell light bulbs door-to-door. I'd put the bulbs in a tattered shopping bag and wear my shabby jacket and ask people if they wanted any bulbs. Most didn't.

My buddy Gene sold light bulbs for decades. He told me years later that if I had dressed in a white shirt and tie and told people, "I have your light bulbs today," and demonstrated that they actually lit up, I might have made more sales.

If I recall, in the seventies, someone organized the "I found it" campaign, teasing passers-by on billboards with the saying, and then, weeks later, adding "I found new life in Christ."

A friend asked me if I would follow-up with telephone calls asking people if they saw the billboards and if they would like some literature on how to obtain this new life in Christ.

I'm not much good on the phone either, encountering a lot of disinterest and only a couple of receptive seekers.

So, as a senior citizen, I was glad to hear about the Global Media Outreach. An associate pastor signed me up, and I received emails from people inquiring about God on the internet. Strangers wrote me from Africa, India or Kansas City.

To initiate the email, seekers indicated one of the choices offered.

One such choice, after a presentation of the Gospel before I got involved, was, "I received Jesus into my life for the first time."

I would write back encouragement to start reading the Bible, engage in conversational prayer with God, and meet with fellow believers.

On the subject line, I'd repeat his or her name, such as "Jorge," and write, "Jorge's most important decision and eternal adventure."

To me, I can't think of any word more profound and potentially either delightful or horrifying than "eternity" or "eternal." I've awakened with a gasp trying to envision its length and breadth of it. Thinking too deeply about eternity can drive one mad.

I truly want an eternal adventure for the newly reborn Christian.

But in writing that encouragement, I am reminded that this applies to me! I've already started my eternal life—my eternal adventure.

Now when daily joys and setbacks occur, I can see them as part of the adventure.

Did the refrigerator die? It's an adventure to see how God helps me remedy the situation. When the temperature drops again and perishable food is rescued, I can rejoice and thank God!

Little bumps in the road crop up every day—it's always something!

Likewise with so many blessings I too often take for granted.

Whoever thought of a journey as an adventure if no challenges existed?

No bumps, no growth.

Otherwise it's a teacup ride in Disney World.

Safe Sects Sense

You make known to me the path of life; in your presence there is fullness of joy; at your right hand are pleasures forevermore. (ESV)

I like the way *The Message* says it as well:

Now you've got my feet on the life path,
    all radiant from the shining of your face.
Ever since you took my hand,
    I'm on the right way. (MSG)

Upshot

Notice "there is" and "are"—not "will be." It's already happening!

70 Don't knock it until you try it

I went to grade school with a kid who wanted jelly sandwiches every day. His mom thought otherwise.

He wanted his jam; she insisted on protein.

They compromised, and for years he ate the same kind of sandwich each day with no variety: liverwurst and blackberry jam—in the same sandwich.

To each his or her own.

Safe Sects Sense

Welcome with open arms fellow believers who don't see things the way you do. And don't jump all over them every time they do or say something you don't agree with—even when it seems that they are strong on opinions but weak in the faith department. Remember, they have their own history to deal with. Treat them gently. Romans 14:1 (MSG)

Upshot

Later in life I have used that principle. Dad thought it was a good idea to drink apple cider vinegar in a glass of water.

I can't stand the taste, and so I add lemon juice and a drink flavor-sweetener like strawberry-watermelon, grape or raspberry. I used to get a flavor with Stevia, but it's hard to find.

Not bad!

71 Navy: How to drink coffee (or not)

I never developed a taste for coffee until I was about 50, when I discovered it could help me stay alert. The folks drank lots of it. In his younger days, Dad would add three heaping teaspoons of sugar.

When the doctor told him to cut it out, Dad started drinking it unadulterated.

I started by adding sweetener or flavored creamers.

In my later years I became acquainted with a retired Navy master chief neighbor. He taught me to drink my coffee "regular Navy." He drank his black, because in the Navy he'd go to the mess and the sugar and powdered cream looked terrible—spattered and caked with someone else's coffee. No, thanks.

Safe Sects Sense

We all have different preferences. Ours are not necessarily better than anyone else's.

Upshot

When I first drank coffee, I did so to stay alert during my 60-mile drive to Air National Guard duty early on a Saturday morning. Unfortunately, my bladder strained to hold out that long. I began taking caffeine pills.

One sunny morning on the way to duty, I noticed a woman leaning out the passenger window to take a picture of Mount Rainier, gloriously displayed.

Inspired and excited, I thought I was on the mountaintop! Full of joy and resolve, I decided to conquer the world at work that morning. I started praising the Lord for energizing me.

Then it hit me.

"Lord, I got that wrong—sorry about that. I'm on a chemical high."

Then, around 15 years ago, my heart started fluttering. Concerned, I asked my wife to take me to urgent care.

After an electrocardiogram, the doctor asked me, "What have you had to drink today?"

"Well, let's see, a big cup of coffee for breakfast, fast food for lunch with Diet Coke and a couple refills, another Diet Coke with dinner...."

"Too much caffeine can trigger atrial fibrillation."

I thought about the four caffeinated drinks I normally took to work. Yup. I was overdoing the culprit.

I've cut back to one a day—if that.

72 Playing hooky

On a whim in second grade, for no apparent reason, I decided to leave school. I walked toward home.

Suddenly, it dawned on me that arriving home at noon would defy explanation.

A large log graced the grassy vacant lot next to our house. I decided to hide out by lying down next to the log.

With thoughts of the consequences of my crime of being absent without leave, I couldn't sleep. With no watch, I had no idea what time it was.

I let my imagination run away with me, and I endured an interminable, everlasting afternoon. School let out at 2 p.m., and finally, I thought it was at least 3 or 4 and safe to go home.

I walked through the door at 2:05.

"How did you get home so quickly?" Mom asked.

"Uh, I got a ride."

It never happened again. I wasn't about to self-inflict that much torture.

Safe Sects Sense

O Lord, you have examined my heart
  and know everything about me.
You know when I sit down or stand up.
  You know my thoughts even when I'm far away.
You see me when I travel
  and when I rest at home.
  You know everything I do.
You know what I am going to say
  even before I say it, Lord.
You go before me and follow me.
  You place your hand of blessing on my head.
Such knowledge is too wonderful for me,
  too great for me to understand!
    I can never escape from your Spirit!
  I can never get away from your presence!

If I go up to Heaven, you are there;
  if I go down to the grave, you are there.
If I ride the wings of the morning,
  if I dwell by the farthest oceans,
even there your hand will guide me,
  and your strength will support me.
I could ask the darkness to hide me
  and the light around me to become night—
  but even in darkness I cannot hide from you. Psalm 139:1-12
(NLT)

Upshot

God pursues you and me wherever we might go or hide. God has been described as the Hound of Heaven in a poem by Francis Thompson. My friend, Jim Nardo, startled me with his prayer, appealing to "The Hound of Heaven, the Great Golden Retriever."

73 Salvation on the installment plan?

Call me an Evangelical-Covenant-Nazarene-FM-Bapticostal. I've worshiped all over the world.

Some say Protestants, by their many denominations, are too divisive. Don't fool yourself. Catholics and other religions find plenty to argue about.

Rather than division, I've found unity and much common ground wherever I worshiped.

Where some debate may come is in the area of a Second Blessing.

I don't get too wrapped around the axle on that.

One friend made up a little jingle:

I'm a happy, happy, happy Nazarene
I'm a happy, happy, happy Nazarene
I've been to the altar twice
And I thinking I'm awfully nice
I'm a happy, happy, happy Nazarene

I personally think most denominations teach some form of the Second Blessing.

Pentecostals call it the Baptism in the Holy Spirit with the initial evidence of speaking in tongues, with more spiritual gifts to come.

Nazarenes also call it the Baptism in the Holy Spirit, resulting in what they call entire sanctification, or freedom from original sin which, in turn, frees one from subsequent deliberate sin.

Nazarenes, however, think of sin as John Wesley defined it, as discussed elsewhere in this book.

Both Pentecostals and Nazarenes emphasize the need for a second trip to the altar, following the initial trip for salvation.

Baptists and others teach about subsequent trips. They might call such experiences consecration, recommitment, dedication, fully surrendering [the rest of] one's life to Jesus.

The Church of God, Cleveland, Tennessee, puts a third term to use, teaching salvation, baptism of the Holy Spirit and sanctification.

Wayne Grudem comes up with an interesting solution in his *Systematic Theology*. I commend his book to you for all the many shadings of meaning, but he suggests that Pentecostals, charismatics, and cessationists alike drop the term "Baptism in the Spirit" as a departure from the New Testament meaning and agree on the universal use of an infilling of the Holy Spirit.

Citing instances in the Bible of infillings with and without accompanying tongues, he concludes as follows:

> Yet an even more commonly used term in the New Testament is "being filled with the Holy Spirit." Because of its frequent use in contexts that speak of Christian growth and ministry, this seems to me to be the best term to use to describe genuine "second experiences" today (or third or fourth experiences, etc.). Paul tells the Ephesians, "Do not get drunk with wine, for that is debauchery; but be filled with the Spirit" (Eph. 5:18). He uses a present tense imperative verb that could more explicitly be translated, "Be continually being filled with the Holy Spirit," thus implying that this is something that should repeatedly be happening to Christians. Such fullness of the Holy

Spirit will result in renewed worship and thanksgiving (Eph. 5:19 – 20), and in renewed relationships to others, especially those in authority over us or those under our authority (Eph. 5:21 — 6:9).

In addition, since the Holy Spirit is the Spirit who sanctifies us, such a filling will often result in increased sanctification. Furthermore, since the Holy Spirit is the one who empowers us for Christian service and gives us spiritual gifts, such filling will often result in increased power for ministry and increased effectiveness and perhaps diversity in the use of spiritual gifts....

There should be no objection at all to people coming into churches, and to encouraging people to prepare their hearts for spiritual renewal by sincere repentance and renewed commitment to Christ and by believing that the Holy Spirit can work much more powerfully in their lives. There is nothing wrong with teaching people to pray and to seek this greater infilling of the Holy Spirit, or to expect and ask the Lord for an outpouring of more spiritual gifts in their lives, for the benefit of the body of Christ (see 1 Cor. 12:31; 14:1, 12).

In fact, most evangelical Christians in every denomination genuinely long for greater power in ministry, greater joy in worship, and deeper fellowship with God. Many would also welcome increased understanding of spiritual gifts, and encouragement to grow in the use of them.

If Pentecostal and charismatic Christians would be willing to teach on these things without the additional baggage of two-level Christianity that is implied by the term "baptism in the Holy Spirit," they might find a new era of greatly increased effectiveness in bringing teaching on these other areas of the Christian life to evangelicals generally.

Safe Sects Sense

> Bear with each other and forgive one another if any of you has a grievance against someone. Forgive as the Lord forgave you.
>
> And over all these virtues put on love, which binds them all together in perfect unity. Colossians 3:13-14 (NIV)

Upshot

One of my late, great pastors, Tommy Paino, resolved the matter by teaching on the "Baptism of Power," thus smoothing over the debate on terms.

74 Who's the Dad of Solutions?

I remember a time when not just a few, but many friends and family members had serious problems.

I had tried to calm the fears of sons and daughters as the dad of solutions. But so many problems from so many directions seemed overwhelming.

My buddy, Dan Koser, provided just the remedy.

"You have the capability to solve any problem in the world," he advised.

"You just can't solve everyone's problem."

I recall reading more good advice:

"Don't teach your Sunday School kids to be like David and fight their Goliaths. Tell them that David is a type of Jesus. Teach them to have Jesus fight their Goliaths."

It's not me, after all. Your God is the Dad of Solutions.

Safe Sects Sense

Be anxious for nothing, but in everything by prayer and supplication with thanksgiving let your requests be made known to God. Philippians 4:6 (NASB)

Or as *The Message* puts it:

Don't fret or worry. Instead of worrying, pray. Let petitions and praises shape your worries into prayers, letting God know your concerns. Before you know it, a sense of God's wholeness, everything coming together for good, will come and settle you down. It's wonderful what happens when Christ displaces worry at the center of your life.

75 Who's as righteous as you?

Bob George, in his book, *Classic Christianity*, told of a conversation with his son. He assured his son of his love, and then asked him if he felt accepted by his dad.

The shocking answer was "no." The son felt loved but perceived he couldn't live up to his dad's intensive life of devotion or sharing the gospel with the same enthusiasm, despite promptings and examples from his dad.

Do you feel both love and accepted by Christ?

Bob further clarified the issue when he spoke at a seminary and asked the seminarians some disturbing questions.

How many of you," I asked, "are as righteous and acceptable in the sight of God as I am?" Every hand in the auditorium was raised. "How many of you," I asked again, "are as righteous and acceptable in the sight of God as Billy Graham?" This time about half of the audience raised their hands. "How many of you are as acceptable and righteous in the sight of God as the apostle Paul?" There were around 10 percent of the hands raised. "Now here's the really tough one," I said. "How many of you in the sight of God are as righteous and acceptable as Jesus Christ?" Only three hands were raised out of an entire auditorium of seminary students.

If you are a true Christian, then you are as righteous and acceptable in the sight of God as Jesus Christ!" You should have seen some of their faces! I think some of them feared that lightning would strike me on the spot! What's your reaction? If you are as shocked as many of those students were, then it may be that you just don't know who you are in Christ. It may be that you know a great deal of doctrine, but your daily Christian life is still more a burden than a blessing.

You may have tried and tried to change your life without success, in spite of all the seminars, books, and websites you have searched. Whatever your situation, I have great news to share with you. Let's look at some of the fantastic inheritance that we have received in Jesus Christ. It's my prayer that you will never again wrestle with doubts about God's acceptance of you, so that you can go on to discover the immeasurable wonders of His love.

Most Christians, I find, understand the general idea behind forgiveness: God took our sins and gave them to Jesus. But that's only half the message! God also took Christ's perfect righteousness and gave it to us! Second Corinthians 5:21 says, "God made Him who had no sin to be sin for us, so that in Him we might become the righteousness of God." How could I stand up and declare that in the sight of God I am as righteous and acceptable as Jesus Christ? Because of what I do? No way! It's because of who I am in Christ.

Try these questions on your family and friends. You may be in for quite a surprise. But if we are genuinely followers of Christ, it's a profound truth we can take to the bank.

And the grave.

And beyond.

Safe Sects Sense

Could having the righteousness and acceptance as Christ be what our Lord was talking about when he said this? "I tell you the truth, of all who have ever lived, none is greater than John the Baptist. Yet even the least person in the Kingdom of Heaven is greater than he is!" Matthew 11:11 (NLT)

76 What if you just can't believe?
A reasonable lifestyle proposal

Someone asked a man, "Are you a Christian?"
"No, but I'd like to live next door to one."
One who genuinely seeks the truth about God and his Son, Jesus, will surely find what he or she is looking for.
Three examples of people I know:
One young man, raised by Christians, went to college thinking of himself as an atheist. Alone in his room, he felt a meaningless emptiness in his life.
He prayed, "Lord, I don't know if you exist, but if so, I want to invite you into my life."
Jesus responded, and the man ultimately became a missionary.
Two others found success in life. One became student-body president of a large high school and then held the same office in Bible school. He married a devoted Christian young lady.
Some eighteen months after graduation he turned to his wife and confessed that he didn't think he was actually a Christian. Oh, he knew the jargon. Everyone thought he was a Christian, but he realized, after all, that he wasn't. The couple prayed together, the man made things right with our Lord, and he became a dynamic Christian teacher and organizer of prayer breakfasts, Bible studies and a large evangelistic crusade.
Another successful man worked his way to the top enlisted grade in the military. One day he realized he hadn't surrendered his life to

Jesus and ultimately settled the matter with the Lord and sought baptism in the church where he had served on a number of projects.

Served?

Both these men had "gone through the motions" and accomplished good works in the church. They had good examples in their wives.

They had acted like disciples.

Their wives had followed Jesus' Great Commission: "Go therefore and make disciples of all nations, baptizing them in the name of the Father and of the Son and of the Holy Spirit." Matthew 28:19

My point: if at first you have difficulty believing, act like a disciple of Jesus. The lifestyle is unsurpassed, with boundless opportunities for phenomenal friends, fulfilling, meaningful service to humankind and good, clean fun.

A disciple keeps reading, studying, asking, and eventually listens to the "still, small voice" of God and, with a compelling, heartfelt pull of the Holy Spirit, yields his life to Christ's glorious salvation.

Is that you? Let's get on with it!

Safe Sects Sense

The late, great Dallas Willard says many churches put too much emphasis on evangelism and not enough on making disciples, in compliance with the Great Commission which, after all, is for everyone's own good. He says make the primary focus discipleship, and evangelism will take care of itself.

Upshot

As the old hymn says, "If you want joy, real joy, wonderful joy..." Here I'll alter the next part a bit:

Be a disciple.

Make a disciple.

77 2001—an earthshaking year

Something big shook up people in Western Washington the year of 9/11. An earthquake with a 6.8 magnitude caused significant damage.

I stayed home sick from the Corps of Engineers that day. I was talking to Dan Koser on the phone when the house started shaking. I crawled under the desk, and the TV on the piano fell to the floor.

Fortunately, our home was well-built and sustained no serious damage. But authorities closed the Corps building, and when I called to learn of any releasable news, I could reach no one.

My counterpart public affairs officer in Walla Walla, "Dutch," called me at home to offer any help he could muster. He suggested patching me into each of our dams to determine any damage or downstream threat.

One by one, he enabled me to talk by phone to someone at each of the dams. They reported no damage.

Then Dutch said he could send out a news release to Seattle media if I would draft a report.

I did so and emailed him the draft. Dutch took off his own Walla Walla District letterhead logo and changed it to the Seattle District of the Corps of Engineers.

Finally he dispatched the news to Seattle broadcast and newspaper outlets.

Safe Sects Sense

And my God will supply every need of yours according to his riches in glory in Christ Jesus. Phil. 4:19 (ESV)

Upshot

I recall many times when I felt isolated and alone, or wondering what to do next. It was then that God sent me just the resource, person or idea that resolved the situation perfectly.

Between marriages, I felt such isolation. It was then that God sent my best Air Force buddy, J.B., to offer ample time, counsel, encouragement and comfort. Praise God for timely help just when I need it!

78 Maybe we don't know as much as we think

I found fascinating the response of a theologian who was asked to convince skeptical college students and professors of the existence of God.

He asked the professors how much of the whole history of knowledge did their students know. They admitted that of all there is to know, none knows very much.

The theologian then proposed that they use 3 percent as a starting point, although all suggested it was far less.

He then made the case that if one doubted the existence of God, perhaps the knowledge skeptics lacked—the other 97 percent—unlocked any remaining mysteries about God. That if they explored that 97 percent of all knowledge in history, God's existence would be beyond all doubt.

Safe Sects Sense

For just as the heavens are higher than the earth, so my ways are higher than your ways and my thoughts higher than your thoughts. Isaiah 55:9

Upshot

While the theologian had a clever way of trying to convince skeptics, I believe that God has revealed everything we need to know about him and his Son, Jesus, in his Word, the Bible. And the Bible is the most documented and verified book of all ancient literature, with thousands of manuscripts affirming the accuracy of the original inspired writings.

And yet, what amazes me about the Bible is that my knowledge ever expands the more I read it.

79 Rescue the perishing

Deployed to New Orleans by the Corps of Engineers following Hurricane Katrina, I waited in line to check out at a nice Walmart Super Center. I remarked to a resident how big and new the store looked.

"This store has been all over the media after the hurricane," she said.

Walmart had invited community members to come in and help themselves to perishable items following a power outage.

People obliged by helping themselves to perishable TVs, stereos, cameras, iPads, drugs and boom-boxes.

The pharmacy remained closed, but I observed that business now thrived in the other departments.

Safe Sects Sense

The Bible makes it clear that God forbids stealing, except in one situation, but even that has a penalty.

People do not despise a thief if he steals to satisfy his hunger when he is starving. Yet if he is caught, he must pay sevenfold, though it costs him all the wealth of his house. Proverbs 6:30-31

Upshot

I guess Walmart ran out of boom-boxes. And not just in New Orleans. Deployed in 2008 to Albuquerque, a thief broke into our mini-van behind a nice hotel and took my boom-box. My bad. I had no business leaving it in plain sight.

80 O for a helicopter on the volcano!

Wifey and I hiked into a volcano on the Big Island in Hawaii on a hot day. Park rangers warned us to take four bottles of water each, but foolishly we thought one each would suffice.

We got so close that we could feel the heat of the lava under our feet, and we could see red-hot lava slowly moving within 20 to 30 feet from us.

I had saved my water for my wife, only to learn later she had saved hers for me.

Suddenly on the hike back, everything went white. I had heat exhaustion.

Fortunately, rangers nearby saw our dilemma and gave me water and electrolytes to drink.

I remarked that I'd give $500 for a helicopter ride back to port.

A ranger told me that a man broke his leg there a week earlier. It took rangers 30 minutes to reach him and another 40 minutes for a helicopter to reach him to fly him to a hospital.

Price tag: $1,900.

Uh, that's OK, I think I'll walk back!

Safe Sects Sense

"But don't begin until you count the cost." Luke 14:28

Upshot

Hydrate, people! More recently, Suzanne and I went shopping. She said she felt dizzy.

A good friend advised us to go get checked out at the heart hospital. Dizziness in women sometimes indicated a heart problem.

After a couple hours in the emergency room, the doctor gave her a clean bill of health, warning that she suffered from dehydration.

She has had no recurrence and has taken care to drink ample amounts of water.

81 Keep your left hand to yourself, but how should we greet someone?

In 1991, the Air National Guard deployed me to Jeddah, Saudi Arabia, escorting a Spokane TV news crew to interview airmen preparing for war as part of Desert Shield.

I received a cultural orientation—what to do and not to do while in-country. Saudi's for example, consider it an insult to show the sole of your shoe to a person. Don't do it.

Likewise, one should never touch another person with the left hand, which must be used only for the dirtiest of jobs.

I've remembered that advice decades later. Now I instinctively reach for a doorknob with my left hand and try to keep my right hand clean. It's a good habit to keep.

We do well to learn the best other cultures have to offer.

Safe Sects Sense

...they gave the right hand of fellowship to Barnabas and me... Galatians 2:9 (ESV)

Don't be afraid, for I am with you. Don't be discouraged, for I am your God. I will strengthen you and help you. I will hold you up with my victorious right hand. Isaiah 41:10 (NLT)

Upshot

Our home group, led by Gene Neudigate, rehearsed a scripted skit to present to the church congregation. I couldn't resist a bit of mischief and, as each of us held onto our scripts to begin the actual performance, I added an unexpected introduction to the skit. Knowing Gene's self-consciousness in front of an audience, I fulfilled the scripture, Romans 16:16, to "greet one another with a holy kiss." I planted a smooch on Gene's cheek, to the uproarious laughter of the audience

Discombobulated, Gene, red-faced, tossed the pages of his script in the air.

82 The joke's on him

An Air National Guard captain had tried to perfect a tradition among the senior staff. Every time a visiting general officer attended the meeting for the first time, he had coached the staff altogether to loudly holler a profanity-laced welcome.

The usual protocol when the brass entered called for someone to yell, "Gentlemen, the commander." Or, "Ladies and Gentlemen, General Throckmorton." Everyone stands at attention.

The captain had a different version. I'll clean it up: It sounded something like, "WELCOME, YOU BIG, UGLY FUNGUS-FACED TOAD-SUCKER!!!"

The captain lived in excited anticipation for any opportunity to arrange the welcome for the next high-ranking visitor.

He didn't have to wait long. He heard that a general was on his way, expected to pop in at any moment. He reminded the staff of what to holler in unison.

Someone got wind of the plot and planned an even better prank. The secretary called the captain out of the meeting.

The senior staff got their instructions amended, and the captain returned a couple minutes later.

Presently, the door opened and in walked the expected general officer.

"WELCOME, YOU BIG, UGLY FUNGUS-FACED TOAD-SUCKER!!!"

Oops. The captain alone had shouted the greeting while everyone else remained silent.

Safe Sects Sense

Mom always warned us that horse-play would result in someone getting hurt. Consider the chance that a prank can backfire.

83 What I want my children and grandchildren to know – the top 20

1.　You are loved far beyond what you know.

2.　Your (step) mom/grandmother/great grandmother and I love you exponentially more, empowered with super-love because of the love God has shown us by giving his own Son to die in our/your place.

3.　Tell me about what it is about God you don't like. I probably don't believe in that god either.

4.　I have never known a mortal's love more than the love Suzanne K. Harris shows me and you.

5.　Your mom/grandmother said she'd take your place in Hell if it would save you!!!!

6.　No good work that you or I could ever do could earn our way to Heaven.

7.　The most satisfying, exciting, joyful life anyone ever had is by pursuing Christlikeness.

8.　No sin you could ever commit (other than permanently rejecting Jesus) is beyond God's forgiveness.

9.　There is nothing your mom/grandmother and I value more than the desire to spend eternity with you.

10.　What does one value so much as to sell one's soul to the devil?

11.　If someone intends to surrender his or her life later in life, is the delay worth the risk of dying tomorrow?

12.　Every objection or alternative you have to biblical salvation has a reasonable answer.

13.　Why would a good God allow suffering?

　　a. God won't rob us of free will. Robotic love doesn't exist. You must choose to accept (and act to build) love.

　　b. We live in a fallen world with people choosing evil over good.

　　c. Suffering not only leads to success, it causes people to turn to God. A former drunk in our men's group is often asked to pray for alcoholics. He prays,

"Lord, help them to hit bottom, where he can finally seek help." Someone has said there is no progress without suffering and no success without failure. My own life, and those of millions of others, proves it.

    d. I have observed in seven decades how suffering inspires people to band together to provide care and relief.

14.   Someone may have told you that Christianity is "exclusive." On the contrary, other religions are exclusive, because they say you must regard Jesus Christ from their perspective, or you are an infidel.

15.   Christianity is unique because it doesn't say that only Christians deserve to go to Heaven. Rather, that no one deserves to go to Heaven, because we have all done wrong during our lives (Romans 3:23). We can gain admittance to Heaven by repenting of our wrongs, accepting Jesus Christ's death as payment for our wrongs and deciding to follow and worship him as Lord. The principle is that Jesus is the only way to God, not any particular church or denomination (John 6:40). Thus, salvation is accessible to everyone and is intended by God for everyone: believers "from every nation, tribe, people and language" will be saved (Revelation 7:9). Thus, far from being exclusive, Christianity is inclusive. Anyone who chooses to accept Christ as Lord and Savior is a Christian and has equal standing with all other Christians before God. (Adapted from *Rational Christianity*)

16.   Christianity is unlike others because of the necessary and sufficient evidence of the resurrection and the empty tomb.

17.   There is no greater or more serious risk or potential joy in the history of the universe than one's choice between accepting or rejecting eternal life with Jesus.

18.   A life with Jesus results in far more gain, starting here and now, than anything you think you might do without.

19.   So we're not giving up. How could we? Even though on the outside it often looks like things are falling apart on us, on the inside, where God is making new life, not

a day goes by without his unfolding grace. These hard times are small potatoes compared to the coming good times, the lavish celebration prepared for us. There's far more here than meets the eye. The things we see now are here today, gone tomorrow. But the things we can't see now will last forever. 2 Corinthians 4:17-18 (MSG)

20. The greatest fulfillment and joy you could possibly attain in life is to trust Jesus to empower you to live your life as he would live it if he were you! "I have been crucified with Christ. My ego is no longer central. It is no longer important that I appear righteous before you or have your good opinion, and I am no longer driven to impress God. Christ lives in me. The life you see me living is not 'mine,' but it is lived by faith in the Son of God, who loved me and gave himself for me." Galatians 2:20 (MSG)

[Disclaimer: I lovingly and respectfully request your letting me know if you've found the full assurance of the timeless standard of a better worldview.]

84 Key to civil discourse

Some years ago, a personal evangelist came to our church. He told us how to share the Gospel as he did with thousands of individuals. After each question, he responds, "I see."

He said to keep the issue in the other person's court.

He asks such questions as these:

Do you have any kind of spiritual belief?

To you, who is Jesus?

Do you think there is a Heaven and a Hell?

If you died right now, where would you go?

If what you believe were not true, would you want to know?

On the last question, Bill says he's never gotten a final "no." Then he often lays an open Bible on the person's lap and asks them to read Romans 6:23.

"What does that mean to you?"

If the answer is bizarre, he asks them to read it again.

Then he has them read Romans 10:9-10. Same process.

Finally, he asks the person if he or she would like to make things right with God and invite Jesus into the person's life.

I have tried to apply this in countless situations in life.

Asking questions.

What an ingenious way to defuse emotion with volatile issues.

Safe Sects Sense

"Ask, and it will be given to you; seek, and you will find; knock, and it will be opened to you." Matthew 7:7 (NIV)

"If any of you lacks wisdom, you should ask God, who gives generously to all without finding fault, and it will be given to you. But when you ask, you must believe and not doubt, because the one who doubts is like a wave of the sea, blown and tossed by the wind. That person should not expect to receive anything from the Lord. Such a person is double-minded and unstable in all they do." James 1:5-8 (NIV)

Upshot

My friend Dick Osburn served as department head for an oil company in Alaska. Fellow executives wondered why he seemed to get more money for his department than other departments.

Dick revealed the key to me, and I've adopted it as one of my mottos.

"Asking is free," he said.

85 Moses' sin and God's merciful, jolting surprise

I love it when an author jolts me!

Reading Jon Courson's *Application Commentary*, OK, I already knew God's penalty to Moses kept him out of the Promised Land. God told Moses to speak to the rock, but Moses got mad and struck the rock.

Moses got angry at the people. In some translations, Moses called them "rebels." But Courson points out that in the Greek Septuigint, the word is *moros*, from which we get "moron."

"You morons, must we fetch you water?"

Secondly, Moses sinned by taking credit for what only God could do.

Then Moses sinned by mischaracterizing God, saying God was angry at the people when it was Moses himself.

I'm delighted when I find Christ in the Old Testament.

Moses struck the rock and the Rock was Christ! "For they drank from the spiritual rock that accompanied them, and that Rock was Christ." 1 Corinthians 10:4 (NIV)

Courson points out some amazing symbolism: Moses had previously stuck the Rock. Christ was struck once, and on the cross, his one sacrifice was sufficient. But Moses struck the Rock again, and that was a bridge too far.

So, Moses died without going into the Promised Land.

And here's where the delightful jolt comes in!

Courson: "Your mercies are new every morning," the prophet proclaimed (Lamentations 3:22, 23)…Moses could not enter the Promised Land. But God is so merciful and gracious that 1,500 years later, who stands on the Mount of Transfiguration in the Promised Land? Moses himself (Matthew 17:3).

God snuck him in!

Safe Sects Sense

You and I must never test the mercy of God by pushing the envelope of sin, seeing how much we can get away with. Even so, we can never underestimate how high, wide and deep is his surprising mercy!

Oh the deep, deep love of Jesus
Vast, unmeasured, boundless, free
Rolling as a mighty ocean
In its fullness over me
Underneath me, all around me
Is the current of your love

Leading onward, leading homeward
To your glorious rest above
　　--Audrey Assad

Upshot

Mom taught us as kids with the song: "Deep and wide, deep and wide, there's a fountain flowing deep and wide."

And "Wide, wide as the ocean, high as the Heaven above, deep, deep as the deepest sea is my Savior's love! I, though so unworthy, still am a child of his care; for his Word teaches me that his love reaches me everywhere!"

86 Too hush-hush and sacred to mention?

Don't get me wrong. I think we don't show enough reverence for God.

On the other hand, I'm told to "come boldly to the throne of our gracious God. There we will receive his mercy, and we will find grace to help us when we need it most." Hebrews 4:16 (NLT)

In the Old Testament, common people couldn't even touch holy things or go behind the curtain to the Holy of Holies.

Then, Jesus became our one sacrifice and God tore that curtain from top to bottom and invited us into his presence.

And so it startled me when someone in a church swore me to secrecy in order to hear an utterance from God.

The secret, she said, precluded repeating it for its sacredness.

O my. Now what?

She told me the utterance, and I kept it to myself.

For awhile.

But then I saw the sacred utterance on Baptist reader boards outside churches.

Here it is. I think it's good enough to tell everyone we know:

"I called you to be fishers of men, not cleaners of fish. You catch 'em. I'll clean 'em."

Read and heed.

Safe Sects Sense

What I tell you now in the darkness, shout abroad when daybreak comes. What I whisper in your ear, shout from the housetops for all to hear! Matthew 10:27 (NLT)

Upshot

I heard about an elderly woman who eagerly looked forward to going home to Heaven, climbing in God's lap and giving him a hug.

A wise man responded, "Isaiah looked up and saw the Lord. Angels flew back and forth saying, HOLY…HOLY…HOLY.

In the sacred moment, Isaiah, struck with his own inadequacy in God's presence, could only say, "Woe to me!" I cried. "I am ruined! For I am a man of unclean lips, and I live among a people of unclean lips." Isaiah 6:5

The wise man telling the story concluded, gently:

"And you want to climb up in God's lap?"

87 I can say 'amen' or 'O me'

Living in two states, I get to attend four or five men's groups.

In one of them, a brother confessed that he had trouble thinking well of a former member who exhibited a great deal of pride.

Our brother went to the Lord about this proud man.

The thought came to him—was it from the Lord?

"It takes one to know one."

We all struggle with pride. It's one of my daily confessions:

"Lord, forgive my selfish pride."

Safe Sects Sense

Again, Mark Vroegop, our Indiana pastor, preached a sermon on pride. He opened in prayer.

"Father, show us our pride. A proud person doesn't always know he's proud."

88 Gotta know the military jargon

In the military you don't want to get on the wrong side of the cook, the paymaster or the person in charge of duty assignments.

In the Air Force, the joke was that one's best assignment—base—was the last one or the next one. Somehow the present assignment never made the list.

I used to say in the Air Force and Army Corps of Engineers that human relations and the finance officer had a "yes" book and a "no" book.

When the Air Force found that it had too many captains left over from the Vietnam era, I got a "Dear John" letter and severance pay.

I applied for a federal civilian job, but my career field at that time allowed no new applicants.

It seems exceptions usually apply. But too often I didn't know the hidden language or secret handshake.

Apparently the Lord put his thumb in someone's back and I got the magic phrases:

The government would accept my application if included the words, "Within 90 days of discharge" and if I persuaded a hiring supervisor to submit a "by-name request."

It "just so happened" that a civilian teaching position became available at the Defense Information School at Fort Benjamin Harrison, Indiana, where I was serving as an Air Force officer.

The Navy boss knew me well, and he gladly submitted the vacancy paperwork requesting my name.

My other book, *Treasure Trove in Passing Vessels*, tells the miracle of my transition from military to civilian.

Suffice it to say that God enabled the joyful acceptance of the job. The magic phrases played a role.

Learning them was a God-sighting.

Safe Sects Sense

For the LORD God is our sun and our shield. He gives us grace and glory. The LORD will withhold no good thing from those who do what is right. Psalm 84:11 (NLT)

89 Should you and I use a Bible commentary?

Dad used Bible commentaries, and Dr. Roy Swanstrom, head of the Seattle Pacific University history department, called Dad one of the best Bible teachers he had heard.

Others have recommended against commentaries, suggesting one read a quality Bible translation and take the time to meditate on passages to determine God's message directly, relying only on cross-references to other passages on similar topics. The idea: God wanted to speak directly to the children of Israel, but the people wanted Moses to be an intermediary. Reading commentaries, even of godly men and women, could be see as using intermediaries.

And yet, some people who don't use commentaries will readily read books by Christian scholars—aren't they commentaries?

I've found commentaries helpful, especially to enlighten me on cultural expectations and failures during Bible times.

For example, the glorious commentary on a woman announcing the Resurrection—unthinkable if one were making it up. Commentaries informed me of the low place of women in those days. Women couldn't testify in court.

Having a woman announce the greatest event in history—the Resurrection—can only mean one thing.

It was true!

Safe Sects Sense

I heard some great advice about study Bibles with commentary.

"The words at the top shed a lot of light on the words at the bottom!"

Upshot

If you vote "no" on commentaries, please think long and hard, meditate and then enlighten me on the following passage:

"At Parbar westward, four at the causeway, and two at Parbar." 1 Chronicles 26:18

90 That's offensive! Maybe not

It seems that the nightly news tells about someone or everyone offended by something.

One of the best books I've read recently is *Unoffendable* by Brant Hansen. He tells about his own struggle with rude drivers and day-to-day activities of others that offended him. He decided that being offended didn't help his blood pressure or well-being, and he looked for ways to overcome being offended.

He found a number of Bible verses such as Proverbs 19:11 "Good sense makes one slow to anger, and it is his glory to overlook an offense."

As a result of his research and prayer, fewer and fewer matters offended him, and so he wrote the book. See Chapter 101 in my book (it's at the end of this book).

Problem: It's still possible to offend me, although perhaps not quite as much as before.

In addition, when I tell people about the book, they initially tend to resist, sometimes citing my own past situations in which I was offended.

Human nature is to cherish our right to retaliate when someone hurts our feelings! We don't want to give up the chance to lash out at someone who, we feel, did us wrong.

Here's how I've settled this in my own mind: followers of Christ start a journey the day they invite Jesus into their lives. It's a lifelong spiritual journey called sanctification to become more and more like Christ.

As we progress on that journey, God can empower us to be less and less offended.

At this point, someone might object that no one has met a person who is unoffendable.

Initially, I thought this was a "gotcha" objection. Many people I know occasionally fly off the handle, more or less, when they are offended, and count me in that number, as I think over the past 74 years.

Then God started showing me people who have overcome being selfishly offended.

Names upon request!

Safe Sects Sense

The question comes to mind: picture yourself further down the road when you have nearly attained Christlikeness; would a fully Christlike person be offended by traffic and insults? I don't think so.

Good motto to live by: First assume positive intent.

Good attitude to maintain: I live on the mountaintop, but I'm not always home. [Actually, Heaven is our home. We live now in a temporary residence.]

Upshot

You may have thought of Jesus turning over the money-changers' tables. Was he offended? Not selfishly. Yes, he had righteous indignation.

Should we be righteously indignant?

Dallas Willard says that few of us are adequately equipped to follow through with righteous indignation.

But, as a Bible teacher reminds me, God equips those he calls to carry out one of his assignments.

For years, I've enjoyed the *Life Application Bible* and now the *Chronological Life Application Bible*.

It challenges me in the commentary on Numbers 25:10-11 about anger:

"Ask these questions when you become angry: (1) Why am I angry? (2) Whose rights are being violated (mine or another's)? (3) Is the truth (a principle of God) being violated? If only your stakes are at stake, it may be wiser to keep angry feelings under control. But if the truth is at stake, anger is often justified, although violence and retaliation are usually the wrong way to express it....If we are becoming more and more like God, we should be angered by sin."

91 God-sightings

If you knew me as a teenager, you have every right to think of me as hard-hearted. I'm reluctant to admit this, but even Bible characters revealed their dark side.

You could say I rode on the short bus in high school. The bus that went to Ballard, near home, also transported mentally challenged pupils.

To our shame, my buddies and I teased those unfortunate kids. They would compose disjointed riddles, and we would imitate their voices and make up similar come-backs. We'd laugh and they'd stare at us, not sure whether they should laugh or not.

Thinking back, those kids exhibited consistent sweetness and joy. I was too immature to acknowledge their cheery disposition.

I call that the dark side of the first half of my life.

Later, as I invited God increasingly into every area of my life, a miracle happened.

God removed my hard heart made of stone and replaced it with a heart of flesh. More and more, the jeers lessened and something holy appeared in their place.

Many times now, I know when God is moving.

It's when the tears flow.

Safe Sects Sense

And I will give you a new heart, and I will put a new spirit in you. I will take out your stony, stubborn heart and give you a tender, responsive heart. Ezekiel 36:26 (NIV)

Upshot

He must become greater and greater, and I must become less and less. John 3:30

92 Pickpocket

Jack Barron has more than begun his ninth decade, and his wife Linda calls him "Type A," meaning he's like the Energizer Bunny.

In his late 70s he researched a trek across the Atlantic and a wild trip through Spain, Italy, France, England and Iceland, all in six weeks.

He researches well, but the trip for the four of us, dragging nine bags up and downstairs at train stations, likely would fit more the strength and energy of a 17-year-old!

I had been most of those places before, but I agreed to go mainly because I had missed two earlier opportunities to go to Normandy to see the anniversary of D-Day. This was to be near the 70th anniversary. When I had lived in Germany in 1984, several public affairs specialists in my office helped set up the 40th Anniversary visit of President Ronald Reagan. Rats! I would have loved being there.

Years later, Wifey found a cruise of the British Isles. I resisted, having seen the United Kingdom.

"Oh, but they're stopping in France to let people visit Normandy!"

I consented. But on the ship, several days into the cruise, the captain announced a dock strike in France and we would not stop there. Nuts!

So in 2014, I determined to get there.

First the youthful six-week trek. Our ship landed in Barcelona. On the subway, two women pushed hard against me to get on the train as I tried to get off.

I reached down and noticed my wallet was missing from my front pocket. The younger of the two pushy women had taken it.

I hollered, "My wallet is missing!"

Passengers, apparently fed up with the pickpocket reputation, pulled the emergency cord, spotted the wallet, grabbed it away from the thief and handed it out to me.

Then a passenger yelled in English, "There they are!" The two women stepped off.

My heroic wife held onto the purse of the younger woman as I started shouting, "Policia! Policia!

The older woman, apparently trying to discipline the younger, started slapping her junior silly.

Suddenly, three plainclothes police officer showed up. They told us it would take two hours to make the trip to the police station to press charges.

Instead, I sat down with the young women, gave her a tract, told her Jesus and I forgave her and said my peace.

"Go and sin no more."

Safe Sects Sense

Be merciful, even as your Father is merciful. Luke 6:36 (ESV)

Upshot

Should we look the other way when we encounter sin? No, we must do what we can to minimize sin's grip on individuals and society. Sin usually has consequences. We must remember that justice is getting what we deserve. Mercy is not getting what we deserve. Grace is getting what we don't deserve.

93 What is your royal, priestly, prophetic calling?

Most of us aim low. I know I have. We don't want to come off as arrogant or proud. Preachers rightly tell us God isn't looking for someone who has it all together. He's looking for a broken, humble, meek (not timid) person.

But in God's high calling of us followers of Christ, he gives us the titles and duties of prophet, priest and king.

Who me?

We must first resist the notion of lording it over "commoners." Jesus himself provides the supreme model of how prophets, priests and kings should serve—with love, compassion and empathy.

Looking at Exod 19:4-6, "God had a reason for rescuing the Israelites from slavery. Now he was ready to tell them what it was: Israel was to become a kingdom of priests and a holy nation where anyone could approach God freely and they would represent God to the rest of the world. It didn't take long, however, for the people to corrupt God's plan. God then established Aaron's descendants from the tribe of Levi as priests (Lev 8–9), representing what the entire nation should have been. But with the coming of Jesus Christ, God has once again extended his plan to all believers. We are to become holy, 'royal priests' (1 Pet 2:9). The death and resurrection of Christ has allowed each of us to approach God freely." –*Chronological Life Application Bible*

It gets even better, if we look at the entire message of the Bible in context. Timothy Keller notes the following:

Prophet, Priest, and King—"All of these facets of ministry are brought together in 1 Peter 2:9. Here we are told that followers of Christ have been made kings and priests–'a royal priesthood'–that we 'may declare the praises of him who called you out of darkness,' which is the work of a prophet. The Spirit equips every believer to be a prophet who brings the truth, a priest who sympathetically serves, and a king who calls others into accountable love–even if he or she lacks specialized gifts for office or full-time ministry. This Spirit-equipped calling and gifting of every believer to be a prophet, priest, and king has been called the *general office*. This understanding of the general office helps prevent the church from becoming a top-down, conservative, innovation-allergic bureaucracy. It helps us understand the church as an energetic grassroots movement that produces life-changing and world-changing ministry–all without dependence on the control and planning of a hierarchy of leaders."

Keller further explains:

"The kingly general office is one of the reasons that many denominations have historically given the congregation the right to select its own leaders and officers, with the approval of the existing leaders (Acts 6:1-6). In other words, the power of governing the church rests in the people. Though pastors and teachers are uniquely called to build up the body into spiritual maturity (Eph. 4:11-13), every Christian is called to help build up the body into maturity by "speaking the truth in love" to one another (Eph. 4:15). The kingship of every believer also means that every believer has the authority to fight and defeat the world, the flesh, and the devil (cf. Eph. 6:11-18; Jas 4:7; 1 John 2:27; 4:4; 5:4)."

– Timothy Keller, Center Church: Doing Balanced Gospel-Centered Ministry in Your City (Grand Rapids: Zondervan, 2012), 344-46.

Safe Sects Sense

It makes sense daily to review our three roles. Are we lovingly calling ourselves and others to account and demonstrating consistent, tender firmness of leadership in our communities and families, willing to fight and defeat the world, the flesh and the devil as our royal duty? Are we speaking the truth in love declaring his praises as prophet, and do we sympathetically serve as priests, assisting seekers to access the very throne room of God?

Upshot

Every year the Corps selected a new group of employee applicants to participate in 12 months of study and field trips to learn leadership qualities. After a few years, it seemed as if the majority of employees had completed the program. The colonel—commander and district engineer—observed that he could not promote each one into a management position. He told graduates to lead in any role in which they found themselves. Many took him at his word and became leader-clerks or leader-secretaries—office managers.

One outgoing woman took on the role of morale officer. Not one of the many celebrations occurring in the building succeeded without her masterful touch.

94 Guarding the temple

I often say that had my name appeared in the Bible—no, not that David—a certain downside risk occurs. Not only my good works but my failures would grace the pages for all to see over thousands of years. OK, look at King David as an example, good and bad.

Even so, I sometimes think about what role I'd like in the Bible. Then I came across I Chronicles 26 and learned some of the Levites became gatekeepers, or temple guards.

Temple guard. Upside and downside. Mom challenged me after retirement to apply at the new Walmart Supercenter in Poulsbo. The interviewer acknowledged my master's degree, my 40-year work experience and offered me a 25-cent raise on the spot—to $8.25 an hour—and made me a people greeter in the garden department. Boring.

Temple guards likely had some dreary days, but wow! What a privilege to draw near to God's house.

As I thought about this, a thought occurred to me. Could it have come from God?

"You are a temple. Guard it."

Astoundingly good advice! God's Word tells me I am the temple of the Holy Spirit, as is the church. I need to guard it. Guard my body-temple from toxic consumption, or the wrong amount, both physically and spiritually. Do my part to guard the church from diabolical attacks.

I have my work cut out for me.

Safe Sects Sense

Do you not know that you are a temple of God and that the Spirit of God dwells in you? If any man destroys the temple of God, God will destroy him, for the temple of God is holy, and that is what you are. 1 Corinthians 3:16-17 (NIV)

So then you are no longer strangers and aliens, but you are fellow citizens with the saints, and are of God's household, having been built on the foundation of the apostles and prophets, Christ

Jesus Himself being the corner stone, in whom the whole building, being fitted together, is growing into a holy temple in the Lord. Ephesians 2:19-22 (ESV)

95 Long-lasting wounds following a rush to judgment

I'm changing the names to protect the innocent. I'm also changing the description of the technique so that I don't tempt youngsters to try it.

Junior high boys, friends of mine, practiced a dangerous passing fad. Or call it a passing-out fad. A boy would instruct the "victim" to breathe a certain way and at the proper moment, someone would grab the obedient one's chest in a certain place to make him pass out.

The father of one of the boys gave him strict instructions to avoid such horseplay—either as the perpetrator or the guinea pig.

Several friends of mine had gathered, not to perform the forbidden prank, but just being typical boys—light punching, wrestling, hammer-locks—what boys do.

The boy's father happened to arrive home and saw the boys tussling. The first thing that came to his mind was that his son was participating in the very thing he knew not to do.

The dad grabbed his son, took him indoors and starting whipping him with his belt.

Now, truly, the son had pulled misdeeds from time to time that deserved punishment, but not for that. His father clearly rushed to judgment, and his son never forgot it. To add insult to injury, he was now the laughing stock of his friends. The pain smarted long after the sting of the belt.

He resented it for years to come.

Safe Sects Sense

"In Deuteronomy 13:12-16, a town that completely rejected God was to be destroyed so as not to lead the rest of the nation astray. But Israel was not to take action against a town until the rumor about its rejection of God was proven true. This guideline saved many lives when the leaders of Israel wrongly accused three tribes of falling away from their faith (Joshua 22). If we hear of friends who have wandered from the Lord or of entire congregations that have fallen away, we should check the facts and find the truth before doing or saying anything that could prove harmful. There are times, of course, when God wants us to take action—to rebuke a wayward friend, to discipline a child, to reject false teaching—*but first we must be sure we have all the facts straight.*" –Chronological Life Application Bible

Upshot

Take caution of the fine line between gossip and fact-finding. Christians have been guilty of sharing gossip "so that you can pray about it."

96 Only one Pappy

My children and grandchildren have brought me much joy along the way. Oh, sure, what family hasn't had their disagreements, disappointments and challenges? But memories of laughter, sharing, problem-solving and even tears have been worth it all.

I have had the additional joy of taking on a blended family, and although I first hesitated, I'm so glad I applied for membership. Once again the great hymn comes to mind, "Plunge in today and be made complete."

That's my story. I am fulfilled.

Oh, it's tough that several are so far away. I didn't much like that they moved. But I have only myself to blame—moving from place to place in the Air Force, and later to Germany as a federal civilian, I guess I taught them that moving was OK. Some example was.

But O what memories.

Gary comes home from Montessori School and announces that he learned about a rhombus. Rhombus? What's a rhombus? I got an "A" in geometry, but I had to look up Gary's new word.

Then seeing Julie the gymnast and taking a picture of her doing a flip, upside down, with her head barely missing the ground…and

Tami so radiant after I financed contacts and new clothes…and Michael tackling the couch and making crowd noise with his mouth…and Jennifer saying, "my daddy is not Pinocchio-pied"…or Ashley calling that restaurant in the sky the "Space Noodle"…Or Kristen looking like Cindy Lou in *The Grinch that stole Christmas*…or bringing the doll house that Grandma Verna refurbished to Emma and Lili in Hollywood…or Austyn naming her exotic fish "Scorch" and being asked how many grandfathers she had. "Lots, but only one Pappy"…or Brenna being called "Sugar Cakes," and responding, "I not Sugar Cakes. I Beezy!" And it stuck! And after seven delightful granddaughters, the thrill of getting my first grandson, Charlie Joe.

Finally—am I that old?—welcoming two great granddaughters, Lauren and Harper, and hearing that at age 3, Lauren's response when she falls:

"I'm OK! I'm OK!"

Safe Sects Sense

I see many of my loved ones far less often than I wish. They and we move around the country. Yet, I am of all men most richly blessed.

97 All that is within me

Proselytizing in the workplace flies in the face of federal regulations. I could hold a Bible study during lunch, and I could talk to someone about the Lord off the clock. But Uncle Sam, or your employer, is not paying us to preach. Instead, do your job, the one for which you're getting paid.

Even so, people somehow knew to come to me for spiritual insight during a crisis. One morning I arrived at work at the Corps of Engineers to find a woman from the finance section crying in my office. Her co-worker the night before had gotten a ride to the hospital for what was to be a routine heart procedure, but he died on the operating table.

"Would you conduct a lunchtime memorial service?" Gladly, I made the arrangements.

Later, our office hosted a national conference in Seattle, which included a luncheon. People had already started to eat, and someone from headquarters came up to me and asked me to give the invocation.

I took the microphone and said something like this prior to offering a prayer:

"In the military, the food was so bad, we prayed after we ate!"

Safe Sects Sense

Years later, I learned of the perfect scripture to use if we delay prayer until people have started eating. It is Psalm 103—"Bless the Lord, O my soul, **and all that is within me**, bless his holy name!"

98 Two more bricks in the Kingdom

I've mentioned elsewhere of a pearl of great price, of a profound solution to life. It has to do with trust.

But I believe two other factors have impacted my life in unexpected ways. Tomorrow I could know tragedy or heartache, but up to now, I haven't known the searing emotional pain that some have known because of tragic loss. But I have known the overwhelming pain of "the double-death of divorce." I've often wondered why God has spared me from terrible accidents and even more earthshaking deprivation. Have I already paid my dues? My future is in his hands, and I cannot do less than to trust him.

I must warn you that you cannot bargain with God. People do as I do and still may suffer terribly. I'm just going to suggest two things you can do, and they may not alter unpleasant circumstances now, but they will result in eternal rewards.

I've said that your eternal adventure isn't something that starts when you die. You're already in eternity.

But when you meet Jesus, what you've done on earth can result in rewards, the Bible says, if good works are done properly, with humility and seeking to carry out God's assignments—effort, but not with the selfish motive of earning.

The two practices that I find of great benefit are giving and praise.

Give off the top from your first fruits, give more than you think you can give, give above and beyond just money—your time and effort as well. You cannot outgive God.

And praise. Spend time each day praising God, not so much for what he gives you, but for who he is—Creator, Sustainer, Judge, Redeemer, Love, Mercy, Grace… You can think of dozens of his attributes and character. "Lord, You are my Righteousness." Try writing them down.

That's it! Not only will giving and praise change your attitude and outlook, but you'll make a difference both now and for eternity.

Safe Sects Sense

God made him who had no sin to be sin for us, so that in him we might become the righteousness of God. 2 Corinthians 5:21 (NIV)

If anyone speaks, they should do so as one who speaks the very words of God. If anyone serves, they should do so with the strength God provides, so that in all things God may be praised through Jesus Christ. To him be the glory and the power for ever and ever. Amen 1 Peter 4:11 (NIV)

Bring your full tithe to the Temple treasury so there will be ample provisions in my Temple. Test me in this and see if I don't open up Heaven itself to you and pour out blessings beyond your wildest dreams. Malachi 3:10 (MSG)

Upshot

Dad taught from his research that giving to the storehouse, as some translations read, traditionally meant the universal, global church. We should look after the needs of the local church and community, but not neglect worldwide needs as well.

99 Who is your Moses and Joshua?

I have many that I look up to as examples. Besides my parents and grandparents, I think of Pastor Wally Roseberg. He married later in life, but I knew him as a tall bachelor who prayed two hours every morning and lived his life every moment as a tribute to our Savior.

More recently, another great example was Tommy Paino. My friend Gene said that our former church taught us the law, but Pastor Tommy taught us about grace.

When Gene was troubled and alone, Tommy said, "Gene, if you wake up in the middle of the night with your troubles, call me, and we'll meet at an all-night coffee shop."

When someone else went through troubled waters, Tommy offered to pay out of his own pocket for a Christian counselor.

Both of these men I considered my mentors, my Moses. Just like Joshua, Moses' assistant for many years, learned from the great leader of the Israelites and became Moses' replacement.

Well-trained, Joshua led God's people into the Promised Land.

Safe Sects Sense

Think of your Moses. If that person is still alive, express your gratitude.

Upshot

Having learned from your Moses, who is (or should be) your Joshua? Someone needs to learn what you learned. Pass that wisdom along, and develop one of tomorrow's leaders.

100 Do opposite

"I can't stand Seinfeld's George Castanza, my wife said.

"Something would be wrong with you if you liked him," I responded. Writers crafted his disgusting personality into the script. Even his TV gym teacher had nicknamed him "George Can't-Stand-Ya."

George personified failure—in employment, love and life.

One day, he decided that in everything from now on to do opposite of what he felt. His first test: he insulted a woman.

To everyone's amazement, the woman smiled and affectionately grabbed his arm. Off they went. After that, every opposite impulse expressed resulted in positive experiences—a new life for George.

Years ago I heard a preacher say that human nature virtually always is opposite of how God wants us to respond. Is this true?, I thought.

Since then, I have found yes, it is so.

When my natural impulse is to respond to anger on the road or at home, the Spirit is standing by, eager and ready to empower me to respond with peace, gentleness and kindness.

Do I observe an idiot driver cutting me off? The Spirit wants me to plead the Blood of Jesus on behalf of him or her, and I often pray accordingly. Becoming more like Christ involves disciplining myself to do opposite of my natural impulses.

Mark Vroegop, my Indiana preacher, expressed concern that we often may give the wrong impression to those inquiring about salvation. We may inadvertently lead them to the notion that life will be so wonderful as a Christian that it's like ascending on an up-escalator.

It's not at all like that, he warns. It's like fighting our way up the down-escalator, bumping into people, encountering temptations—"STOP!"—being inundated by obstacles, impediments, enticements to slide back. "NO!" Keep going. Endure. Fight. Persist. Keep moving upward—until you reach the top.

Do opposite. Not like George.

Safe Sects Sense

Like St. Paul.

Upshot

Like the audience of One

101 St. Paul picked up sticks?

Recently we visited the Legacy Bible Church in Noblesville, Indiana, and one verse made the trip worthwhile, triggering thoughts of my own spiritual legacy: *"...Paul had gathered a bundle of sticks and laid them on the fire..." Acts 28:3*

What?, the pastor, Dr. Keith Kunda exclaimed. A preacher or evangelist gathering sticks? My mind flashed back to Tommy Paino and his untimely demise from Lou Gehrig's disease. His associate, Pat Sorum, said it best, recalling her own journey:

Thinking about when I was 16 years old, I wanted to be in the ministry. I didn't consider wanting to be in the ministry the same as having a "call" to the ministry. I believed you had to be "called" to ministry and I was hoping that God would "call" me. I believed "ministry" meant working in the church (Now, after a full career of "ministry" I realize the "call" is more for "you wouldn't do this if you didn't have a 'calling' to do it.") (ha)

After years of religious studies, a degree in counseling, a couple of years of seminary, Jim and I were ready to work in our first church full time. One of our professors was a friend of Tommy and Sandy's of Carmel, Indiana—he recommended us to this new church in Carmel. We were hired and so the learning began.

As I was growing up in church. I always saw pastors sitting on the platform. Many times the chairs they sat on were ornate in some way. To me this meant they were higher than the rest

of us. They were to be more respected, beloved—esteemed, and I liked that.

So jump to one of the first lessons I learned about what it means to be a minister. At this wonderful church we had many fun parties celebrating weddings, anniversaries, birthdays and holidays. After the first one we attended, the crowds were gone and I saw Tommy get down on the floor and start scraping frosting off the church carpet. (I thought to myself, this is odd—won't the janitor do this?) Sandy started cleaning; Jim started putting chairs away.

Me? I was visiting with the few people left in the church. After they left, I went over to Sandy to continue chatting. She said to me, "You don't have a ministry bone in your body, do you?"

This was "ministry"? Cleaning the church after parties? Not my idea of ministry. This is something called "servant leadership." I was soon to see the leadership practices of this couple was—instead of gathering power and position at the top, they led by serving—putting the needs of others first. Jim and I saw this style of ministry modeled for us over and over in the lives of Tommy and Sandy.

We hadn't been at Northview long when a parishioner called me "Sister Pat." I didn't like it so I said to him, "You can call me Pat, Patti, or even 'Hey you' but don't call me 'Sister'. I am not your sister." Well he went to Tommy and told him I had offended him, and he was leaving the church. Tommy called me in. He always started our meetings with a few jokes, and then he told me I had offended this man with my comments and even though I didn't want to be called "sister," it was part of being in relationship with this person and I should apologize to him.

Tommy was a good listener. He assured me he understood me, but then he asked me to honor the relationship more than my personal bias. I didn't like it but I humbled myself and apologized to this man. I didn't realize it then, but I was beginning to learn an important lesson about this "calling" I wanted so badly. It had more to do with humbling myself than sitting in fancy chairs.

Time after time during our years at Northview I took my offenses to Tommy hoping he would start a war for me. He would say to me, "Pat you have to know who your friends are….Don't sweat the small stuff; these things have a way of working themselves out." And you know what? They did.

During holiday dinners Tommy told the staff, "Don't sit with your friends; find someone who is alone and sit with them." This was so counterintuitive for me. But I learned. I have learned that ministry isn't about position, being higher than others, seeking honor. It is about serving, loving people even when we are offended. Walking with the hurting where they are, without judgment, and somehow in that relationship change happens.

Jim and I moved on from Northview but took with us the lessons learned about leading as servants. It transformed our careers as we pastored another church. I approached my career as a counselor as a servant, and now in our job working with troubled kids who are court-ordered to a children's home. We lead as servants. Put the relationship with the child first. Not easily offended, but treasure the relationship above all else. And somewhere in this relationship we begin to see change. Change always starts in loving the hurting. Out of that relationship we tackle problems together.

Each January is the anniversary of Tommy's passing. It is then I am again reminded to say a little thank you for his life well lived.

Tommy Paino III

FOR FURTHER STUDY: Read the whole Bible as a child with no helps, starting with the New Testament. The Bible often explains itself in context. Remember: a text without context is a pretext for a proof text. I'm certainly not against a good study Bible. My favorites are the *Fire Bible* and *Life Application Bible*, both referenced in this book, as well as *Classic Christianity*, by Bob George, mentioned in Chapter 75 of this book. They can provide cultural and doctrinal insights. But the greatest joy comes from your own study, meditating on a passage and asking God how your life can change from what he is teaching you through his unchangeable Word. I grew up in a church whose watchword is "where is it written?" If one has an idea for a doctrine, show us where it is written in God's Word. I've recently discovered *Forensic Faith*, by J. Warner Wallace, which differentiates between blind faith, unreasonable faith and evidentiary faith. Interested in my first book? Look for *Treasure Trove in Passing Vessels*, available at Amazon and elsewhere, in paperback or Kindle. Comments? Email me at SafeSectsGraceandTruth@gmail.com

ABOUT THE AUTHOR

Although Dave Harris is a retired lieutenant colonel in the Air Force (light colonel before breakfast, full colonel after breakfast!), the only identity he cherishes is follower of Christ who happens to live in America. None other is needed. He feels that tribal identity politics divides people rather than uniting them. This is Dave's third book. The first one is *Treasure Trove in Passing Vessels*. The second, no longer in publication, is an audio book on the 100-year history of Christ Memorial Church (now Gateway Fellowship) in Poulsbo, Washington. Dave earned a master's degree in mass communications at Denver University after pursuing a B.A. in broadcast journalism at the University of Washington in Seattle. But his most purposeful and joyful education has been his private studies in biblical research, a pursuit he highly recommends for you.

Made in the USA
Middletown, DE
12 January 2019